# Best Practices in Change Management – 2009 Edition

*575 participants share lessons and best practices in change management*

© 2009 Prosci

ISBN: 978-1-930885-57-8

Acknowledgements

**Editors** – Tim Creasey and Jeff Hiatt
**Study design** – Adrienne Boyd, Tim Creasey, Becky Fiscus, Jeff Hiatt, Ashley McNeal, Avery West
**Data collection, graphs and tables** – Tim Creasey
**Study analysis** – Adrienne Boyd, Tim Creasey, Becky Fiscus, Jeff Hiatt, Judith Larrimore, Ashley McNeal, Allison Seabeck, Martha Wawro, Avery West
**Reviewers** – Judith Larrimore and Kathy Spencer

## Table of contents

The 2009 edition of *Best Practices in Change Management* aggregates the findings from the 2009 study and previous studies to form one of the most comprehensive bodies of knowledge on change management. Any findings that have been brought forward from the 2007 edition of the report are noted with the following text after the findings are presented, "Source date: 2007".

# Tables and figures

# Executive overview

## *Participant profile*

Five hundred and seventy-five participants from 65 countries took part in the 2009 Best Practices in Change Management benchmarking study. This report combines the findings and data from the 2009 study with Prosci's previous five studies to form one of the largest bodies of knowledge related to managing the people side of change.

> 2009 study – 575 participants
>
> 2007 study – 426 participants
>
> 2005 study – 411 participants
>
> 2003 study – 288 participants
>
> 2000 study – 152 participants
>
> 1998 study – 102 participants

Figure 1 shows the geographic distribution of participants in the 2009 study.

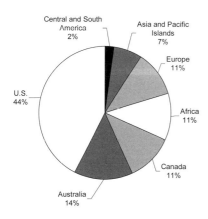

### Figure 1 – Geographic distribution of participants

Study participants represented a variety of job titles within their organizations. The top three job roles of participants were:

- Change management team leader
- External consultant
- Project team leader

## *Study objective*

The objective of this study is to uncover lessons learned from practitioners and consultants so current change management teams can benefit from these experiences. Specific attention is paid to what is working and what is not working in all areas of change management.

The 2009 report also presents emerging trends in change management, looking to identify the changes that have occurred and the future direction of this discipline.

Because change management is a holistic system that requires involvement by change managers, project teams, executives, managers, supervisors and front-line employees, this report details how each of these different groups are engaged in managing change.

### New sections in the 2009 report

New questions were added to the 2009 study to expand the scope and depth of the research. These new areas of focus include:

- Sponsor effectiveness ratings and engagement approaches
- Manager and supervisor ratings, engagement approaches and support
- Team structures and resource allocation
- Proactive resistance management and resistance avoidance
- Project management integration
- Change readiness evaluation
- Attributes of effective communications
- Role of change management in training
- Change Portfolio Management
- Change management trends

## *Study highlights*

### Greatest contributors to success

For the sixth straight study, the top contributor to success identified by participants was active and visible executive sponsorship. The greatest contributors to overall change management success were:

1. Active and visible executive sponsorship
2. Frequent and open communications around the need for change
3. Utilization of a structured change management approach

### Greatest change management obstacles

For the second study in a row, ineffective sponsorship was cited as the greatest obstacle. The most commonly encountered obstacles to change management success included:

1. Ineffective change sponsorship from senior leaders
2. Resistance to change from employees
3. Insufficient change management resources and funding
4. Middle management resistance

### Change management correlation to meeting project objectives

Projects with excellent change management effectiveness were nearly six times more likely to achieve project objectives than teams with poor change management effectiveness. Excellent change management also correlated directly with staying on schedule and staying on budget.

### Use of a change management methodology

Over 60% of study participants used a structured methodology to manage the people side of change. This is nearly double the rate from the 2003 study. The top factors for choosing a methodology included ease of use, previous experience with the methodology and approaches that were "proven to be effective."

### When to start change management

Over 80% of study participants recommended beginning change management activities at project initiation, although less than 40% actually started this early. When change management was started late in the project, employees were more resistant and less engaged, and change management activities had to be adjusted. A directive from senior leadership was the primary trigger for starting change management early.

### Most effective change management tactics

The most effective change management tactics were engagement of the primary sponsor in the change management process (including building a sponsorship coalition), face-to-face communications and involvement of employees in the overall process. The least effective tactic for managing change was the use of impersonal communications such as email.

### What to do differently

Study participants listed the following activities to do differently on their next project:

1. Select and apply a structured change management approach
2. Secure the correct level of executive sponsor and build a stronger sponsorship coalition
3. Create and implement a carefully orchestrated communications plan
4. Start change management earlier in the process
5. Add more full-time change management resources to the team

## Most important sponsor activities

Study participants identified the most critical roles for executive sponsors when leading change:

1. Participate actively and visibly throughout the project
2. Build a coalition of sponsorship
3. Communicate directly with employees

For the third consecutive study, more than 50% of participants reported that their sponsors had a less than adequate understanding of the role of an effective change leader.

## Most common mistakes made by executive sponsors

Study participants cited the biggest mistakes their primary sponsor made during their change projects including failing to personally engage in the project, avoiding direct communications with employees and abdicating his or her role as sponsor.

## Consequences of sponsorship at the wrong level

Participants who had sponsors at the wrong level cited severe consequences to the change and to the organization, including delayed projects, failed changes and resistant employees. Projects with sponsors at the wrong level also had difficulty acquiring resources and meeting project objectives.

## Role of managers and supervisors in times of change

More than 80% of participants ranked manager and supervisor involvement as extremely or very important. The most critical roles for managers included:

1. Communicating with direct reports about the change and why the change is happening
2. Demonstrating support for the change
3. Coaching employees through the change process
4. Engaging with and providing support to the project team
5. Identifying and managing resistance

Overwhelmingly, the two roles that managers and supervisors struggled with most were coaching employees through the change process, and identifying and managing resistance. Only 40% of participants provided formal change management training to managers and supervisors.

## Most common mistakes made by managers and supervisors

The top three most common mistakes made by managers and supervisors were:

1. Not effectively communicating with their employees
2. Actively resisting the change themselves
3. Ignoring the change

## Attributes of successful communications

Participants said that the most successful change messages included what the change meant to employees and why the change was happening. The most successful communicators were senior business leaders who were committed, engaged and passionate about the change, and who were viewed by employees as credible. Face-to-face messages were the most effective, with the preferred senders for change messages being the executive sponsor (the "person in charge") and an employee's direct supervisor.

## What to do differently next time with communications

When asked how they would change their communications approach for the next project, participants said they would communicate more often, engage managers and supervisors more effectively as communicators and start communications earlier.

## Resistance to change

The top reasons that front-line employees resisted change in their organizations included lack of awareness of why the change was happening, a perceived negative impact on their current job role and the past performance of their organization with change.

The reasons that managers resisted change included a lack of awareness of why the change was happening, a lack of involvement in the change process and an increase in workload (lack of time or work overload). Mid-level managers were identified as the most resistant group to change.

Participants stated that much of the resistance they experienced from employees and managers could have been avoided with effective change management.

## Team structure

A majority of study participants reported that a team structure where the change management resources were integrated into the project team was the most effective. The reasons to use an integrated structure included increased project knowledge and shared accountability for success among all team members.

## Change management resources

Study participants reported change management resource levels ranging from two to ten full-time-equivalent (FTE), depending on project size. The average percentage of project resources (in FTE) dedicated to change management was 24%. More than 60% of participants cited having too small of a budget and 47% suggested adding more change management FTE to the project.

## Use of consultants

Forty five percent of participants used an external consultant to support change management work. The top roles played by consultants supporting change management activities were to provide training on change management, to lead the change management effort or to coach the change management team. By a five-to-one margin, participants cited a lack of internal expertise in change management as the primary motivator for hiring a consultant.

## Project management and change management integration

Over 80% of study participants integrated change management activities into their project management activities. However, 40% of participants said their project team did not view change management as important or a high priority. The top tactic to engage project teams was working collaboratively, followed by making a compelling case for why change management was necessary.

## Change readiness

Over 60% of participants took steps to evaluate change readiness, with written assessments, surveys and interviews being the top methods.

## Justifying change management

Over half of the participants had to justify change management to senior leaders, with the most common approach being the use of past failures and the illustration of the negative consequences of poorly managing the people side of the project. Past successes with change management and senior level buy-in were the top conditions that resulted in a team not having to justify change management.

## Enterprise Change Management

Eighty five percent of participants in the 2009 study indicated that their organization was at Level 3 or lower when assessed against Prosci's five-level Change Management Maturity Model. A majority of participants reported that less than one in four of the projects underway in their organization were using change management processes and tools. One third of participants indicated that change management was a requirement for new projects, and 43% of participants indicated they had a standard organizational methodology (up from 29% in the 2007 study).

## Location of change management group

Human Resources was the most common response for where the change management group was currently placed, with the PMO (Project Management Office) being cited as the "best place" for change management expertise to reside in the future.

## Change saturation

Two thirds of participants indicated that their organization was nearing, at or past the point of change saturation. Over three quarters of participants (76%) expected an increase in the amount of change over the next two years.

## Change portfolio management processes

One third of participants kept an inventory or list of all changes underway in their organization, while just under one quarter of participants (24%) had a structured process for managing the portfolio of change.

## Top trends in change management

For the second consecutive study, the top trend identified by participants was a greater recognition of the need for change management within the organization. Change management competency building moved up to the second most prevalent trend in the 2009 study from number five in the 2007 study. The top trends for change management as identified by 2009 participants included:

1. A greater recognition of the need for change management
2. Change management competency building throughout the organization
3. Dedication of resources for change management
4. Use of a structured methodology and tools

# Greatest contributors to success

Study participants identified five areas as the greatest contributors to overall change management success. These five categories matched the results from the 2007 study and included:

1.  **Active and visible executive sponsorship**
    Consistent with the findings from Prosci's previous five studies, active and visible executive sponsorship ranked as the number one success factor for change management programs, with participants citing this factor four times more frequently than any other area. Participants cited the need for senior business leaders to be visible and actively engaged in the change process, accessible to the project team, knowledgeable about the change, committed and involved. Active and visible executive sponsorship included:

    *   Visibility and accessibility throughout the entire project

    *   Proactive identification of key stakeholders to build a sponsorship coalition

    *   Direct communications with employees to build awareness of the need for change and to share the organization's vision and objectives

2.  **Frequent and open communications around the need for change**
    Frequent and open communications included regular information sharing that established a clear and compelling reason for the change. This included identifying impacted groups, building awareness of the need for change and sharing the costs or risks of not changing. Participants cited the need for a "clear line of sight" to the business strategy that was consistent and easy to understand. Study participants also emphasized the need to share how both the organization and end-users benefited from the change.

3.  **Structured change management approach**
    Participants cited the use of a structured change management approach along with a detailed change management plan as a key contributor to their success. Study participants cited the need for practical change management knowledge and a well-orchestrated program that included a clearly-defined process, early change management planning and pre-change analysis (situational assessments).

4.  **Dedicated resources and funding for change management**
    Dedicating resources to change management included the assignment of staff trained in change management for planning and implementation, and the allocation of budget for change management activities. In the case of some large change projects, study participants indicated the need for change management resources to be assigned by function or by region. This enabled change management expertise to be onsite and local to the community impacted by the change (to manage the change at the closest point of impact).

5.  **Employee engagement and participation**
    Employee participation included many types of involvement by employees, particularly focus groups and other activities that allowed employee input to the design of the change. Study participants cited the need for proactive interactions that fostered feedback and resulted in enthusiastic and motivated employees who knew why the change was needed. Study participants in 2009 reported a growing resilience among employees with a noticeable willingness to support needed business changes. Customer input was also cited as an important element for successful change management programs.

Additional contributors to success cited in the 2009 study included:

- Engagement of middle managers and supervisors including skill building and proactive communications

- Effective project management with an integration of change management

- A growing awareness of the need for change management in order for projects to succeed

## Contributors to success over time

The table below shows the ranking of contributors to success over the last six benchmarking studies. Active and visible executive sponsorship ranked number one in each of the six studies. Between the 2007 and 2009 studies, the top five contributors remained the same, although there was some shifting in their order. Participants in earlier studies also included comments on the quality of the team and the drivers of change as contributors to success; these factors have moved off the list of top contributors in more recent studies.

| Contributors to success | 2009 rank | 2007 rank | 2005 rank | 2003 rank | 2000 rank | 1998 rank |
|---|---|---|---|---|---|---|
| Active and visible executive sponsorship | 1 | 1 | 1 | 1 | 1 | 1 |
| Frequent and open communications around the need for change | 2 | 3 | 3 | 4 | 2 | - |
| Structured change management approach | 3 | 2 | 2 | 5 | - | - |
| Dedicated resources and funding for change management | 4 | 4 | - | - | - | - |
| Employee engagement and participation | 5 | 5 | 4 | - | 2* | 2 |

**Table 1 – Contributors to success over time**

* This item was combined with "Frequent and open communications around the need for change" in the 2000 study.

# Greatest change management obstacles

Study participants identified seven main obstacles to the overall success of their change management programs. The top four areas matched the results from Prosci's 2007 study with the exception that "Insufficient change management resources and funding" moved from the number four spot to number three on the 2009 list.

1. **Ineffective change sponsorship from senior leaders**
   Participants cited ineffective change sponsorship as their primary obstacle, specifically stating problems with:

   - Inactive or invisible sponsors

   - Sponsors at the wrong level (not high enough in the organization)

   - Poor alignment among key stakeholders resulting in a weak sponsor coalition

   - Wavering sponsor commitment (especially on longer projects)

   - Conflicts of interest between key business leaders (managers' objectives were not aligned with the change)

   - Little or no access to the primary sponsor by the change management team

   - Unwillingness of the primary sponsor to manage resistance from other managers

   - Mixed priorities and projects competing for limited resources and funds

   - Lack of knowledge by senior executives around their sponsorship role resulting in poor leadership of the change

   - A sponsor who left the position mid-project resulting in poor continuity and reduced leadership support (revolving door of sponsorship)

2. **Resistance to the change from employees**
   Employee resistance to change was cited nearly as frequently as sponsorship issues. Specific areas contributing to resistance from employees included:

   - Lack of understanding of why the change was happening and "What's in it for me?" or "WIIFM"

   - Long-tenured employees unwilling to support the change

   - Loss of control and loss of ownership of work processes

   - Fear of the future state, including concerns over job security

   - Change saturation (employees were overwhelmed by the amount of change)

   - Strong feelings of comfort with the current state

   - Strong resistance from those with the greatest knowledge and expertise on current systems and processes

   - Weak economy driving people away from "non-core" work (avoidance of change projects)

   - Lack of involvement by employees in the change process (no input or participation)

3. **Insufficient change management resources and funding**
   Participants cited a general lack of resources and funding available to conduct the necessary planning and implementation of change management. Specifically, participants said they were:

   - "Working in the margin" trying to do two jobs at the same time

   - Finding it difficult to obtain funding because of competing initiatives

- "Change saturated" (too much change underway at the same time) causing a shortage of both people and money

- Lacking in change management knowledge and skills, or were not the right people for the project

4. **Middle management resistance**
Middle managers were reluctant to support the change and therefore created a major obstacle when:

- The change was not aligned with their operational objectives

- They anticipated negative impacts to their day-to-day operations

- They feared loss of control or power

This lack of support was evident by middle managers who were unwilling to communicate consistent and accurate information about the change and who exhibited poor sponsorship of the change with their employees. Some participants noted that middle managers lacked the knowledge and tools to manage change effectively.

5. **Poor project management**
Participants noted that their change management efforts were disrupted by:

- Project delays and restarts

- Poor definition of the future state

- Scope creep

- Poor planning by the project team

- Shifting priorities

- Lack of clear project goals

6. **Ineffective communications**
Participants cited a number of reasons that their communications were not effective, including:

- Inconsistent messages filtering down through the management chain

- Wrong sender of the change message (the primary sponsor was not available or was unwilling to communicate directly to employees)

- Difficulty reaching employees because of diverse geographical locations or language barriers

7. **A culture that is resistant to change**
Cultural barriers to successful change included:

- A group of employees and leaders who were not receptive to change (or an entire organization that was inherently change resistant)

- A history of past changes that were not successful

- A political bureaucracy or complex leadership structure that interfered with the process of building alignment around the change

Editors' Note: Participants in Prosci's 2005 study also cited cultural barriers to change. They were encountering entrenched organizations that served as shelters for slow responses, entitlement attitudes and complacent employees who were primarily satisfied with the status quo.

# What to do differently on the next project

Participants evaluated what they would do differently on their next project. The findings focused on four areas:

1. Better engagement of senior leaders as change sponsors

2. Improved change management planning and more effective application of change management tools

3. Dedicated resources for managing the people side of change

4. Earlier and more personal communications with employees

## 1. Better engagement of senior leaders as change sponsors

Consistent with the 2007 findings, participants stated they would engage senior leaders earlier and more proactively to:

- Ensure buy-in and alignment around the project

- Obtain sponsorship at the right level in the organization

- Enable senior leaders to participate actively as effective sponsors

Study participants would have created a sponsorship plan and provided more education and coaching for their business leaders around being an effective change sponsor. They cited the need for a strong sponsorship coalition that was aligned around the vision and objectives of the project. They also stated the need for earlier and more frequent meetings with sponsors.

Finally, participants cited the need to engage sponsors in the process of managing resistance with stakeholders. Early resistance management would help the project team create a consistent message and build commitment for the change.

## 2. Improved change management planning and more effective application of change management tools

Participants cited several areas that needed improvement in their application of change management, including:

- Start earlier and improve change management planning

- Conduct better assessments of the change and of the attributes of each impacted group (improved situational assessments)

- Apply a standardized change management process on all projects

- Increase the involvement of employees in the process from the very beginning

- Align change management plans with project management plans

Participants also indicated a greater need for change management training for project team members.

## 3. Dedicated resources for managing the people side of change

Participants indicated that on their next project they would dedicate change management resources and a budget specifically allocated for change management activities. They also recommended careful selection of the change management team, which would become involved with the project sooner.

## 4. Earlier and more personal communications with employees

Participants identified communications as an area for improvement on their next project. Specifically, participants stated that they would use more frequent face-to-face communications and less email. They also stated the need to build awareness around why the change was happening and to create the right level of urgency for the change.

Additional suggestions from project teams included more active engagement of mid-level managers, more training available for employees and faster resolution of resistance.

# Change management effectiveness

## *Correlation between project success and change management effectiveness*

Analysis was conducted correlating change management effectiveness with three dimensions of project success:

- Meeting objectives
- Staying on schedule
- Staying on budget

In evaluating change management effectiveness, participants were provided twelve factors that constituted effective change management (see Table 2) and then were asked to evaluate their overall change management effectiveness on a scale of Poor, Fair, Good or Excellent.

Actual responses vary in the three correlation charts because participants were able to indicate "too early to tell" for each of the project delivery categories. More participants indicated "too early to tell" for meeting project objectives than for schedule or budget adherence.

Figures 2, 3 and 4 show the percentage of projects performing at or above expectations correlated with change management effectiveness using data from the 2007 and 2009 benchmarking studies. For each change management effectiveness category (Poor, Fair, Good, Excellent), the chart shows the percentage of participants who were performing at or above expectations (i.e. those meeting or exceeding objectives, those on or ahead of schedule and those on or under budget).

Projects with excellent change management effectiveness were nearly six times more likely to achieve project objectives than teams with poor change management effectiveness, 95% to 16% respectively. Excellent change management also correlated directly with staying on schedule and staying on budget.

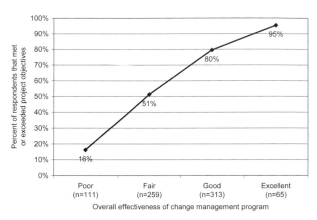

**Figure 2 – Correlation with meeting objectives**

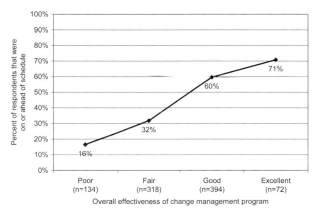

**Figure 3 – Correlation with staying on or ahead of schedule**

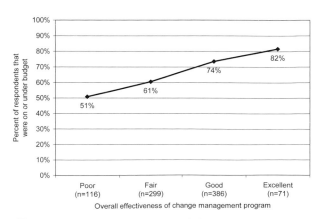

**Figure 4 – Correlation with staying on or under budget**

---

## *Change management effectiveness factors*

The table below shows twelve change management effectiveness factors and the percentage of participants who indicated Strongly Disagree, Disagree, Agree or Strongly Agree for each factor. Participants indicated the strongest agreement with factors 1, 3, 5, 7 and 9, with over two thirds indicating "Agree" or "Strongly Agree." Factors 2, 6, 8, 10 and 12 were the weakest, with nearly one half indicating "Disagree" or "Strongly Disagree." Interestingly, these weaker performing factors included the "resource factor" and the four factors outside of the direct control of the change management team (those that required actions by senior leaders, managers and supervisors).

| Factor | Strongly Disagree | Disagree | Agree | Strongly Agree |
|---|---|---|---|---|
| 1. We applied a structured change management process. | 7% | 22% | 51% | 20% |
| 2. We had sufficient resources on the team to implement change management. | 11% | 38% | 41% | 10% |
| 3. Our change management activities were customized and scaled to fit the change and the organization being changed. | 6% | 18% | 51% | 25% |
| 4. Our change management team had the necessary training and expertise in change management. | 9% | 27% | 47% | 17% |
| 5. We integrated our change management activities into the project plan. | 4% | 16% | 52% | 28% |
| 6. Our business leaders fulfilled their roles as effective change sponsors throughout the entire project. | 11% | 41% | 38% | 10% |
| 7. We implemented an effective communications plan. | 5% | 26% | 50% | 19% |
| 8. Managers and supervisors were engaged in the change and effectively coached their employees through the change process. | 9% | 44% | 41% | 6% |
| 9. We provided the necessary training to employees on new processes, systems and job roles. | 5% | 22% | 56% | 17% |
| 10. Our senior leaders, mid-level managers and supervisors managed resistance to change effectively. | 7% | 44% | 45% | 4% |
| 11. We measured compliance with the change and our overall performance in meeting project objectives. | 6% | 34% | 51% | 9% |
| 12. We effectively reinforced the change with employees through recognition, performance measurement and celebrations. | 9% | 38% | 45% | 8% |

**Table 2 – Change management effectiveness factors**

## *Measuring change management success*

Study participants cited three ways to measure the success of change management:

1. **The degree to which the project met objectives and achieved the desired business results**
   Study participants determined the impact of change management by measuring the project's performance against a predetermined set of metrics (often referred to as Key Performance Indicators or KPIs). These measures included:
   - Financial performance (cost savings or revenue generation)
   - Customer satisfaction
   - Operational performance (quality, speed)
   - Project budget adherence
   - Project schedule adherence

   Study participants emphasized the importance of measuring change management success in terms of overall business results or the degree to which the project met its objectives. Participants encouraged the definition of these success measures at the beginning of the project.

2. **Employee and manager feedback on the change**
   Participants used survey tools, focus groups, assessment instruments and interviews to collect employee and manager feedback. These tools were used to gauge employees' perception of the change, assess employee morale and determine overall organizational readiness. Specific tools that assessed the progress of individuals and groups in the change process were also used. In some cases, participants collected anecdotal stories and testimonials as a way of determining how effectively or ineffectively the change was being implemented.

3. **User adoption and acceptance of the change**
   Study participants developed metrics to evaluate the adoption or acceptance of the

change by employees. User adoption measures included:
- Speed or rate of adoption (by group or by function)
- Ability or proficiency to use new tools or processes
- System usage performance (collected through usage reports)
- Compliance measures

In a few cases, participants measured how well their change management activities avoided or mitigated the negative consequences that can occur during change. Measurements included employee turnover, number of employee and customer complaints, and productivity loss.

## *Change management effectiveness*

In the 2007 and 2009 benchmarking studies, participants commented on their overall change management effectiveness. Comparing the data from the two studies, the percentage of participants reporting "Excellent" and "Poor" change management programs did not change. A greater percentage of participants reported change management effectiveness of "Fair" in 2009 than in 2007, with the number reporting "Good" decreasing (Figure 5).

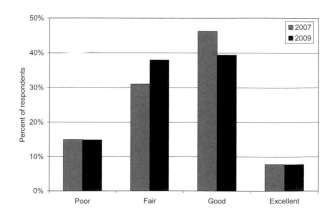

**Figure 5 – Change management effectiveness**

# Methodology

## Use of methodology

For the fourth straight study, the percentage of participants that reported using a particular change management methodology increased (Figure 6). Over 60% of participants in the 2009 study followed a particular methodology.

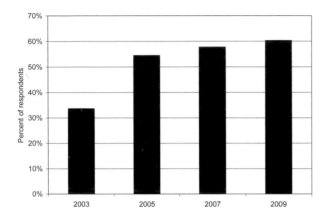

**Figure 6 – Participants using a particular change management methodology**

Overall, participants cited 64 different methodologies they used for change management. Of those 64 different methodologies, 80% of participants cited five common methodologies. In rank order, the most cited methodologies were:

- Prosci or ADKAR
- Internally developed
- Consultant provided approach
- Kotter
- LaMarsh

Editor's note: The change management study invitation was sent to nearly 40,000 members of Prosci's Change Management Learning Center. Because this is not a pure random sample, the rank order of these methodologies may not be representative of a neutral participant group.

## Key factors in choosing the methodology

Those participants who were using a structured methodology shared the key factors in their selection process. The top factors for choosing a methodology were:

1. **Easy to use**
   Overwhelmingly, the top factor for selecting a particular methodology was ease of use. Participants noted:
   - Easy to implement
   - Easy to understand
   - Easy to communicate to others
   - Simple
   - Practical
   - Structured and systematic
   - Logical
   - Comprehensive and holistic

2. **Previous experience with a methodology**
   Many participants cited their own personal experience with a particular methodology as a key factor in selection.

3. **Proven to be effective**
   The methodology chosen was proven and effective, or had been successful when it was applied within the organization previously.

4. **Matchcd the need**
   The particular methodology met the needs of the change that was being introduced and was applicable to that situation.

5. **Flexibility and customization**
   The methodology could be applied to many different types of change and in many different parts of the organization. It was flexible and could be customized to meet the needs of different change programs.

In some cases, participants were required to use a methodology that had already been adopted as the institutional standard and mandated for use or had been provided by the consultant supporting the initiative.

Source date: 2007

## How did you first find out about the methodology you are using?

Participants shared how they were introduced to the methodology they were using. The top four responses were:

- Conducted research on the internet or in the library on "change management"

- Attended a training session within the organization

- Applied the methodology on a change (learned about the process from their own personal experience)

- Learned about change management from an external consultant

Source date: 2007

## When to start change management?

Participants were asked to indicate when change management activities began on the project they were reporting on and when they would recommend starting change management activities. Figure 7 shows the strong bias participants had toward starting change management activities at the initiation of the project. Over 80% showed a preference to begin change management activities at project initiation, although less than 40% actually started this early.

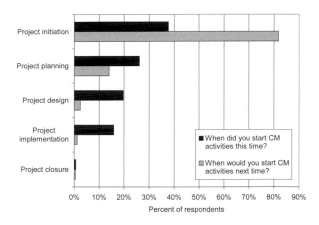

**Figure 7 – When did change management activities begin?**

## Consequences of starting late

Participants who started change management late in the project life cycle commented on the consequences of this approach. The most common consequences of starting change management late were:

1. **Employees were more resistant and less engaged**
   Because change management was not started early, the project experienced higher levels of resistance from employees. People were not motivated to participate. They were not engaged or committed, and they were slow to get on board with the change. Confusion and misconceptions about the change were exacerbated.

2. **Change management activities were limited and ineffective**
   The role of change management was limited and primarily reactive in nature. Participants felt that change management activities were ad hoc, started too late and often limited to only a single change management activity like training or communications. There was too little time to do change management effectively and the work was often rushed. Change management work was isolated from other project work.

3. **Time was spent playing "catch up"**
The change management team had an incomplete view of the change effort including the strategy, direction, expectations and expected benefits. The team expended tremendous energy backtracking and trying to catch up on what had already happened with the project. This effort was viewed as non-value added work and excessively costly.

4. **Change management was not effectively positioned**
There was not support or resources for change management. Roles were poorly defined, and the change management team had a difficult time building relationships, having influence or getting a "seat at the table."

5. **Project design ignored the people side components**
In a number of instances, people issues related to the project design were identified late in the project after change management resources were brought on board. The result was rework and having to revisit project decisions.

6. **Project objectives were compromised**
Benefits were only partially realized or not achieved at all. The project ended up behind schedule or over budget. Results were not sustained.

## Action steps if change management started late in the project

Participants provided the specific action steps they had to take as a result of change management being introduced late in the project life cycle.

Overwhelmingly, the most common action steps cited by participants pertained to adjusting the change management approach. These adjustments included:

- Redo, undo and fast-track communication efforts

- Refocus on building awareness and support

- Work to get sponsor engagement and action (escalate critical issues)

- Limit focus to the most critical activities

- Increase resources for change management

- Expedite change management activities

- Provide education about change management

- Control damage - "put out fires"

- Skip steps or cut corners as necessary

The other action steps cited by participants were:

- Backtrack and learn about project developments that have already occurred (become grounded on project work so far)

- Change the project schedule – put project on hold, push out deadlines, slow down efforts, re-plan or in some cases re-launch the project

- Expend extra time and energy (overall, the team had to work harder)

## Contributors to starting change management early in the project

Those participants who started change management early in the project life cycle identified the factors that contributed to having change management begin at the onset of their project. The top contributors to having change management begin at the onset of the project were:

1. **Senior leadership directive**
Senior leaders connected to the project had a high level of experience with or knowledge of change management. They ensured that change management was incorporated into the project by demonstrating support for change management and insisting that it be adequately addressed. In some cases, senior leaders required change management plans for the project.

2. **Acknowledgement by the project manager**
The project manager or project director recognized the importance of change management and supported its inclusion in

the project. Previous experience with change management by the project manager contributed to this acknowledgement.

3. **Previous experience**
The organization had previous experience with changes where the people side of change was either effectively managed or ineffectively managed. Most responses indicated previous negative experiences where change management was ignored and projects suffered as a result.

4. **Incorporation into project initiation steps**
Change management activities were incorporated into the launch of the project. Participants stated that risk analysis, assessments and stakeholder identification occurred at the launch of the project. Change management activities were incorporated into the project timeline, budget and charter. Change management plans were identified as key deliverables.

Additional reasons for change management beginning early in the project life cycle included:

- The nature of the project itself – including the complexity, perceived difficulty of the change and importance of employee buy-in

- Resource availability – change management resources were available or assigned to the team from the very beginning

- Integration with project management methodology – the organization had taken steps to integrate the change management methodology into its existing project management methodology

## *Most effective change management tactic or activity*

Study participants cited the most effective tactics or activities that were used during their change management implementation. In rank order, the top three were:

1. **Engagement of the primary sponsor and the sponsorship coalition**

Participants listed multiple activities they used to build an effective sponsorship structure for their change including creating a sponsor roadmap, conducting sponsor workshops and having the primary sponsor active and visible. Participants stated that the primary sponsor should be engaged in the process of communicating expectations to stakeholders and aligning the change with the organization's strategy. They should also conduct regular meetings with their leadership team and mid-level managers about the change.

2. **Face-to-face communications**
Participants cited the need for frequent face-to-face communications including road shows, weekly meetings and one-on-one communications.

3. **Involvement of employees in the overall process**
Participants stated that employees should be directly involved in the change process. Examples provided by participants included:

- Cross-functional representation on the project team

- Ongoing dialogue to collect employee input

- Assessments to check the "pulse" of the organization

- Proactive feedback mechanisms

- Effective coaching programs (methods for managers to work with employees on the change and to engage them in the change process)

- Communities of practice

- "Power users" selected by location or function

Editor's note: While sponsorship and communications ranked in the top three most effective change management tactics, participants indicated that these same two areas are the most difficult to perform successfully.

Source date: 2007

## What was the least effective change management tactic or activity?

Participants overwhelmingly reported that the least effective tactic for managing change was the use of impersonal communications. Examples included broadcast emails, intranet sites, videos, bulletin-board postings and newsletters.

Source date: 2007

## What would you do differently next time regarding methodology?

Study participants stated what they would do differently regarding their change management approach. In rank order, they cited:

1. **Methodology**
   Select and apply a structured change management approach.

2. **Sponsorship**
   Secure the correct level of executive sponsor, build a stronger sponsorship coalition and provide more change management training for business leaders.

3. **Communications**
   Create and implement a carefully orchestrated communications plan that more effectively involves senior leaders, uses more communication vehicles and provides more frequent and consistent communications.

4. **Timing**
   Start change management earlier in the process.

5. **Resources**
   Add more full-time change management resources to the team and develop a change management team structure.

Source date: 2007

# Change management activities

Participants described their change management approach by listing the specific actions and steps they completed. The data was divided into three major project phases: start-up (planning), design and implementation. The activities and steps were further categorized according to the primary target audiences:

- Project team

- Managers and business leaders

- Employees

The net result is that the activities and steps participants used can be shown in a 3 x 3 grid, with rows representing project timing (start-up, design and implementation) and columns representing the audience or group (Figure 8).

For each box in this grid, detailed lists of corresponding activities are provided. The labels for each box are intended to be general descriptions for the category and are not intended to stand alone from the activity lists in Tables 3, 4 and 5.

The lists (List A, List B, etc.) referred to in Tables 3, 4 and 5 can be found in the section titled "Supplemental change management activities lists" following the tables.

Editor's note: The Change Management Activity Model shown in Figure 8 was first developed in 2003 and now includes data from the 2003, 2005 and 2007 reports to create a comprehensive view of change management activities across multiple studies.

Source date: 2007

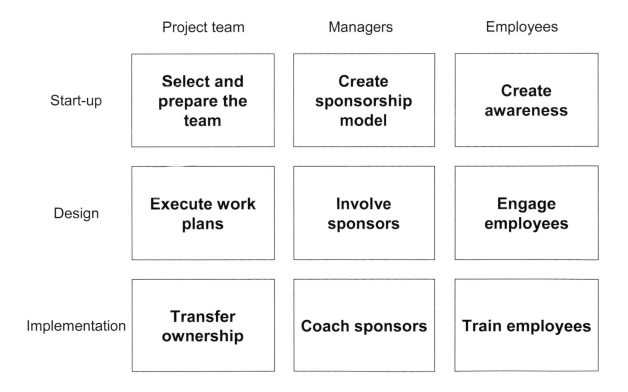

Figure 8 – Change Management Activity Model

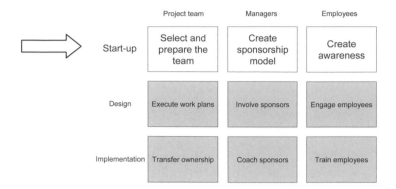

| | with the Project team | with Managers | with Employees |
|---|---|---|---|
| **Start-up** | **Select and prepare the team** | **Create sponsorship model** | **Create awareness** |
| | • Identify the "right" change management team members; consider representation by location or function; use outside expertise when necessary<br><br>• Establish a team structure<br><br>• Train the team on change management methods<br><br>• Understand the nature of the change and the future state; assess the timing of the change (see List A)<br><br>• Define the impact of the change on specific groups; conduct a gap analysis<br><br>• Assess and analyze the current organization (see List B)<br><br>• Create a sponsorship model (see adjacent column)<br><br>• Complete change management readiness assessments (assess culture, barriers and risks)<br><br>• Create change strategies and plans (see List C); develop a schedule and budget; review these plans and get approval from the steering committee<br><br>• Develop change management training for managers and supervisors<br><br>• Integrate change management plans into project management plans | • Identify the required primary sponsor; directly engage his or her support<br><br>• Identify key senior managers and stakeholders throughout the organization who are needed to sponsor the change; assess their current level of support for the change and their competency to manage change<br><br>• With the direct involvement of the primary sponsor, begin building support among all key managers; engage them as active and visible sponsors of the change and ensure alignment with project objectives<br><br>• Form a steering committee for the project (dependent on overall project size)<br><br>• Show managers the current state vs. the future state; create a common view of the nature of the change, why the change is being made and the organization's readiness for change<br><br>• Train senior and mid-level managers on change management and their role as sponsors of change<br><br>• Help create key messages for managers to communicate to the organization (presentations and elevator conversations)<br><br>• Create identifiable actions that senior managers can do to begin supporting the change (see "Sponsor role" section of this report) | • Begin initial communications with employees to create awareness of the need for change and to share the nature of the change (see List D) |

**Table 3 – Team start-up activities**

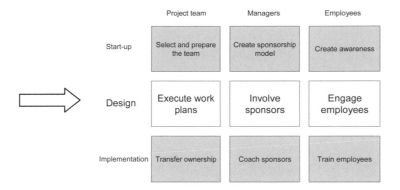

| | with the Project team | with Managers | with Employees |
|---|---|---|---|
| | **Execute work plans** | **Involve sponsors** | **Engage employees** |
| **Design** | • Implement change management strategies (from start-up phase), including specific plans for communications, sponsorship, coaching and training<br><br>• Conduct regular workshops with change agents<br><br>• Identify pockets of resistance and develop special tactics with different groups to counter this resistance<br><br>• Identify job roles impacted; begin to define future skills and competencies for employees; use as input for training requirements and curriculum design<br><br>• Develop coaching and mentoring strategies for front-line supervisors, including development of change management competencies<br><br>• Train the trainers; begin the process of developing internal competency around managing change throughout the organization<br><br>• Hire external resources if necessary to support the change<br><br>• Collect input from customers on how this change will impact them<br><br>• Define measurable objectives (key performance indicators - KPIs) | • Interview all critical senior managers to determine their expectations and desired outcomes; gather input on the change strategy and understand their concerns<br><br>• Maintain regular contact with all senior managers; schedule and conduct frequent and regular meetings; seek their input on critical decisions<br><br>• Conduct steering committee meetings on a regular basis (dependent on project size)<br><br>• Work to develop sponsor capabilities: What do they need to be doing to support the change? How can they best accomplish those goals?<br><br>• Coach sponsors; provide sponsors with a roadmap of sponsor activities and help them prepare key messages; provide coaching on how to share the business vision and the change with employees<br><br>• Identify resistant managers; engage the primary sponsor and other senior managers to address this resistance<br><br>• Seek approval from senior managers at key milestones in the process | • Build awareness around the overall change and why the change is being made (see change messages in List D)<br><br>• Engage employees in the design process; gather input from employees on the design and understand their concerns<br><br>• Use pilots or models to test ideas with employees and to share the future state<br><br>• Use face-to-face meetings to share the vision and strategy<br><br>• Gather employee feedback on the vision and strategy using focus groups and interviews<br><br>• Use question-and-answer sessions, interviews and memos to address employee concerns and share information on a regular basis<br><br>• Demonstrate successes and early wins to employees<br><br>• Share ongoing progress of the design team, including updates to the schedule, so that employees know what to expect and when<br><br>• Continue to answer questions about the personal impact to employees: How will this impact me? How will this change my daily work? How will I benefit from this change? |

**Table 4 – Team design activities**

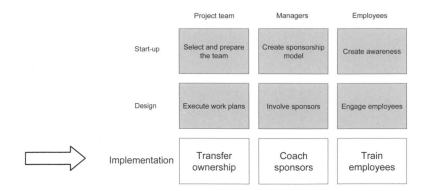

| | with the Project team | with Managers | with Employees |
|---|---|---|---|
| **Implementation** | **Transfer ownership** | **Coach sponsors** | **Train employees** |
| | • Review project progress; monitor activities and measure performance (review KPIs); identify successes and demonstrate short-term wins<br><br>• Adapt change management plans as necessary to address gaps in performance<br><br>• Develop ways to celebrate successes with both managers and employees<br><br>• Create feedback mechanisms<br><br>• Create coaching aides for supervisors to enable them to help their employees through the transition (see List E for "Coaching aides")<br><br>• Begin to migrate change leadership to operational managers<br><br>• Extend team structure to involve local groups in change activities<br><br>• Support local trainers within the organization to implement education and training about the new processes and systems<br><br>• Identify lessons learned and update change management approach and tools | • Engage sponsors in managing resistance (encourage one-on-one intervention)<br><br>• Continue regular and frequent meetings to review progress and performance; update business leaders and senior managers on the solution and the implementation progress<br><br>• Increase the level of senior manager communications with employees (e.g., leadership must stay active and visible throughout the implementation efforts)<br><br>• Provide managers with concrete activities they can perform to support the implementation (provide upward coaching)<br><br>• Report roadblocks to senior managers promptly; resolve critical issues quickly through effective use of the steering committee<br><br>• Use senior managers effectively to manage resistance | • Implement training on the new processes, systems and job roles; align this training with gap analysis completed by front-line supervisors for their employees (include one-on-one training)<br><br>• Listen to employees and value their feedback; move quickly to adjust the design or resolve issues that surface during implementation<br><br>• Provide one-on-one follow-up and coaching<br><br>• Share the critical success factors with employees; audit compliance with the new processes and implement corrective action when needed<br><br>• Assess employees (where are they in the change process?); measure effectiveness of the change management plans and adjust as necessary<br><br>• Quickly identify and address pockets of resistance<br><br>• Celebrate successes and achievement of significant milestones<br><br>• Implement rewards and incentive systems for employees<br><br>• Continue ongoing communications about project outcomes and progress, including specifics about what will happen, when and why<br><br>• When appropriate, tie compensation to performance |

**Table 5 – Team implementation activities**

## *Supplemental change management activities lists:*

### List A – Understanding the future state

- Nature and scope of the change
- Overall timeframe
- Alignment with the business strategy
- Goals of the change
- Reasons for changing
- Risk assessment (risk of not changing)
- The gap between the future state and today
- Who is impacted and how; who is most adversely impacted
- Future state design (if available at this phase) including sample models or scenarios
- What will change; what will stay the same

### List B – Organizational assessment

- Change capacity (How much change has the organization made recently and how much more change can the organization absorb?)
- Change history (What was the effectiveness of past changes and what perceptions do employees have of past change projects?)
- Culture assessment (To what degree do the values and norms of the organization support or oppose change?)
- Change competency (What are the change management skills and abilities within the organization?)
- Authority and capability of primary sponsor (Does the primary sponsor have sufficient power to lead the change?)
- Strengths and weaknesses of the organization related to this change (Overall, what is working in favor of the change and what is working against the change?)

### List C – Strategies and plans

- Change management plan (overall strategy)
- Communications plan
- Sponsor plan
- Training plan (including change management training)
- Coaching plan

### List D – Employee messages

- The current situation and the rationale for the change (why the change is needed)
- A vision of the organization after the change takes place (alignment with the business strategy)
- The basics of what is changing, the nature of the change and when it will happen
- The goals or objectives for the change
- The expectation that change will happen and is not a choice (risk of not changing)
- The impact of the change on the day-to-day activities of the employee (WIIFM – what's in it for me?)
- Implications of the change on job security (will I have a job?)
- Specific behaviors and activities expected from the employee during the change
- Status updates on the performance of the change, including success stories
- Procedures for getting help and assistance during the change

### List E – Coaching aides

- Concrete activities that front-line managers and supervisors can perform to support the change with their employees
- Tools to communicate the new roles and responsibilities to their employees
- Self-assessment guides for employees to assess skill and knowledge gaps
- Resistance assessments and mechanisms to collect feedback from employees during early implementation phases
- Tools to create individual development plans

Source date: 2007

---

# Change management team and structure

## *Team structure*

Data was collected on the change management team structure used by study participants. Participants chose between the two structures shown below or selected "other structure" if their structure did not map to Team Structure A or Team Structure B. In Team Structure A, the change management resources are on the project team. In Team Structure B, the change management resources are external and support the project team.

Team Structure A    Team Structure B

Over 60% of participants used Team Structure A where the change management resources were on the project team (Figure 9).

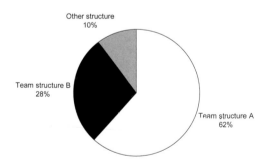

**Figure 9 – Team structures used**

The most common "other" structure cited was a hybrid of Team Structure A and Team Structure B. Hybrid structures included the following:

- The project team itself was responsible for change management.

- Change management was done by a member of the project team with outside assistance including facilitation, coaching, support and advising.

- A single change management group from a company-wide change management office supported and participated with projects in all divisions and departments.

## *Structure preferences*

Participants also expressed which team structure they would prefer and the reasons why.

Advantages of Team Structure A included:

- Increased project knowledge
- Part of the team
- Integrated responsibilities
- Increased credibility
- Ease of communication

Advantages of Team Structure B included:

- Access to leadership
- Objectivity
- Independent from conflicting priorities
- Different scope
- Enterprise approach
- Different skill set
- Elevated status

These advantages are addressed in more detail on the following pages.

## Team Structure A advantages

A majority of 2009 study participants reported that a team structure where the change management resources were integrated into the project team was the most effective. The top five reasons to use an integrated structure were:

1. **Increased project knowledge**
   Change resources inside a project team had a better understanding of the business objectives, context and technical details of the project. They gained the benefit of day-to-day knowledge and were able to monitor events as they unfolded.

2. **Part of the team**
   When change resources were integrated into the project team, they had ownership in the project and shared the team's common goals. They personally engaged and made a commitment to project success. There was an opportunity to build trust through collaboration and involvement in decision making.

3. **Integrated responsibilities**
   All team members shared accountability for the success of the project. Change management resources played an integral role in achieving project outcomes, working with the project team from beginning to end. There was also a need for ongoing and active involvement in change activities from other members of the project team.

4. **Increased credibility**
   Change managers within the project team had increased influence. They were seen as a peer with project-specific knowledge, rather than as an outsider. This position provided increased opportunities to raise people issues, coach the project team and influence strategic direction.

5. **Ease of communication**
   Change resources on the project team were privy to the high volume of communications between project team members. There was no need for a third party relay of information. Change resources could also more directly communicate their change-related information to the project team.

## Team Structure B advantages

A smaller but still significant group of participants responded that the most effective team structure utilized change management resources external to the project team. These external resources took various forms, including subject matter experts (SMEs), resources from a Change Management Office, internal OD consultants or external consultants. The primary reasons to employ resources outside of the project team were:

1. **Access to leadership**
   Change management resources were coaches for sponsors. They were in a better position to manage sponsorship activities when they were external to the project team. The flow of communications between sponsor and change manager was direct, not filtered through a project manager.

2. **Objectivity**
   Resources outside of the project team offered neutrality and an independent point of view. They provided objective feedback and more accurately assessed the people impacts of the project.

3. **Independent from conflicting priorities**
   Change management resources outside of the project team had autonomy to maintain the priority of their change work without being "swallowed by project tasks."

4. **Different scope**
   Participants noted that change management required a specific, constant focus on strategies related to the people side of change. It was a forward facing role with an organizational-level viewpoint that often addressed more audiences than the project itself. Change management also coordinated multiple segments of large projects or programs.

5. **Enterprise approach**
   Organizations with an enterprise-focused change management discipline were able to coordinate many projects and ensure stable, consistent implementation. Resources could be allocated to "hot spots" as needed, leveraging skills across the organization and reducing costs.

6. **Different skill set**
   Change management required specialized knowledge and skills such as experience or training in change concepts and tools, as well as strong communication skills. By contrast, project work often involved a very different set of skills in technical processes or systems.

7. **Elevated status**
   Change management gained a greater level of respect when considered separately from the project team. External change managers reported in at the same level as the project team and were seen as a complementary but equal team. They enabled success by coaching both the sponsor and the project team through the change process.

## Additional team structure considerations

A number of study participants did not indicate a preference between Team Structure A and Team Structure B. Instead, they responded with alternative ideas about the most effective change management team structure.

- The most effective team structure varied from project to project depending on:

  o Nature of the project including size, scope, complexity, impact on people, risk or geographic distribution; responses were equally divided as to which structure was better for which size of change

  o Cultural factors within an organization such as employee response to outside help and fragmentation of groups

  o Resource considerations such as availability of change management skills and experience within the project team and sponsorship coalition

- Hybrid structures. Participants proposed structures that combined resources both internal and external to the project team. These hybrid structures had benefits that included:

  o Balancing project knowledge with outside perspective

  o Change resources within a project had support and expertise from a center of excellence as needed, particularly during busy project stages

  o Allowing for business unit representation while building change skills within the organization

- Entirely unique team structures included:

  o Change management owned by all impacted groups, with involvement from all levels – "everyone in the change circle"

  o Sponsor included in the change management team bubble

  o Change management team positioned hierarchically between the project team and the sponsor

## Decisions on the number of change management resources

Participants identified factors that influenced the number of change management resources on the project as well as those constraining factors that limited the number of resources used.

The top influencing factors were:

- Nature of the change
- Scope of required change management efforts
- Number of impacted groups
- Organizational capacity for change
- Benchmarking
- Geographical distribution
- Phase of project
- Established organizational guidelines
- Strategic importance of the project
- Project team's change management experience

The top constraining factors were:

- Budget

- Availability

- Skill set

- Organizational maturity in change management

- Confidentiality

Influencing factors:

1. **Nature of the change**
   Participants reported that the change itself was a major factor in determining the change management resource requirements. The change characteristics most frequently cited were the type of change (process, systems, reorganization, etc.), the complexity of the project, the number of people impacted and the pace of implementation.

2. **Scope of required change management efforts**
   Resourcing decisions were determined by the amount of change management work to be completed. The scale of the communications plan, training requirements, coaching needs and assessment work were key factors in calculating resource needs. Participants asked themselves, "Do we have enough people to do all the work?"

3. **Number of impacted groups**
   The number of business units, work streams, or levels involved in the change affected the number of change management resources required. Study responses underscored the importance of involving key representatives from each impacted group to answer questions and allow for cross-organizational input.

4. **Organizational capacity for change**
   An organization's cultural acceptance of change and change capacity impacted change management resourcing decisions. Factors such as higher volumes of ongoing change and larger amounts of anticipated resistance resulted in higher resource needs.

5. **Benchmarking**
   Change management resources were allocated based on best practices research, consultant recommendations and lessons learned from past project experiences.

6. **Geographical distribution**
   Projects with global or widely distributed regional implementation required more change management resources.

7. **Phase of project**
   Participants reported that the number of resources needed for change management could vary through the project life cycle. Many noted fewer requirements in the early stages and increasing needs as the project neared implementation. Additional resources were added to projects that fell behind or experienced a lack of progress.

8. **Established organizational guidelines**
   Organizations established enterprise-wide guidelines for making resourcing decisions. These were based on in-house change management methodologies or mandated by a central Project Management Office (PMO), Change Management Office (CMO) or Human Resources (HR) group.

9. **Strategic importance of the project**
   Participants responded that the project's impact to the business was considered in allocating resources. More resources were used in critical or urgent projects and projects with a high risk of failure.

10. **Project team's change management experience**
    The level of change management skill and expertise on the project team, coupled with the team's level of awareness of the importance of change management, factored into resourcing decisions.

Constraining factors:

1. **Budget**
   Nearly 20% of participants cited budget constraints as a primary factor limiting their ability to obtain change management resources. Sponsors and project team leaders were unwilling or unable to pay for change

management resources. Many organizations had no formal budget for change management.

2. **Availability**
   Nearly 20% of participants indicated resource availability as a limiting factor in change management resource decisions. Time and workload constraints on employees, ongoing commitments and conflicting priorities limited the pool of resources available for change management.

3. **Skill set**
   Participants reported a lack of trained and experienced change management resources within their organizations. To be effective in a change management role, resources must not only have technical skills but also soft skills such as teamwork, flexibility and ability to engage a sponsor.

4. **Organizational maturity in change management**
   Resourcing decisions were impacted by the level of awareness of change management within the organization. Lack of buy-in and a low perceived value of change management, particularly at the sponsorship level, resulted in fewer resources.

5. **Confidentiality**
   In several cases, the sensitivity of the project inhibited the number of change management resources.

## Change management lead

When asked who took the lead on change management, the most common responses from participants were the project leader, an individual on the project team, an external consultant or an internal consultant. In a small fraction of cases, an HR representative led the change management work.

Source date: 2007

## Team experience and expertise

Participants evaluated the level of experience and expertise of the change management resources on the project. Nearly one half of participants indicated that the change management resources had less than adequate experience or expertise (Figure 10).

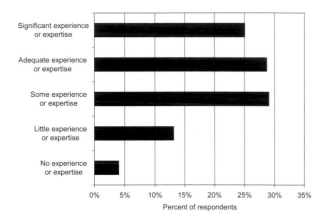

**Figure 10 – Level of experience and expertise of change management resources**

## Building change management knowledge

Participants were asked to identify how they overcame or addressed the lack of change management experience or knowledge in their project. They described the following top five tactics and methods used in overcoming or addressing the knowledge and experience gaps:

1. **Training in change management**
   Change leaders, project team members, managers and sponsors participated in training activities to learn about change management methodologies and strategies. Some attended formal training programs. Others received less formal training through internally developed programs, train-the-trainer programs or ongoing training in regular team meetings.

2. **Coaching and mentoring**
   Coaching and mentoring relationships allowed more experienced change management leaders to provide direction and

support to their counterparts with less change management experience. Some organizations created a formal "buddy system" or shadowing opportunities to allow inexperienced individuals to work alongside experienced team members. Experienced team members took the lead in projects by setting a personal example and offering advice and guidance one-on-one.

3. **Self-study**
Many participants sought out change management knowledge on their own through independent study and research that included reviewing training materials, books, published materials and benchmarking information. Internet-based resources such as online tutorials and webinars were referenced frequently. Participants also cited learning on the job through trial and error and addressing issues as they arise as a self-study tactic.

4. **Engaging consultants and external resources**
Hiring external resources or consultants helped to fill gaps in expertise and supplement full-time employee knowledge. External resources provided support through delivery of training programs that emphasized competency building. Consultants worked to provide knowledge transfer through coaching and strategic advice and, in some cases, even built a change management methodology for the project.

5. **Peer-to-peer networking**
Support groups and communities of practice provided avenues to communicate with other professionals in the field. These networking opportunities allowed for knowledge sharing, collecting of lessons learned and liaising with the leaders of similar projects. More informally, asking questions and fostering open dialogue with other departments that had relevant expertise (communications, training, etc.) helped to address gaps in change management knowledge.

## Change management training throughout the organization

Study participants were asked to recommend the number of training days for change management teams, senior leaders, managers and project teams. Their recommendations were:

- **Change management teams:** three to five days of change management training

- **Senior leaders:** one half to one day of change management training

- **Managers and supervisors:** one to two days of change management training

- **Project teams:** one to three days of change management training

Source date: 2007

## Advice for new change management teams on resources and structure

Participants cited a number of recommendations they would provide to new change management teams about team structure. The top recommendations provided by participants were:

- **Ensure appropriate sponsor access**
Participants mentioned the need for more direct, unfiltered access to the primary sponsor. A number of participants cited the importance of having a team member with the time, credibility, level and respect to effectively coach sponsors.

- **Select the right team members**
Participants provided a number of suggestions for team composition. They recommended a team that had:

  o A wide range of individual competencies, including communications and training skills

  o General experience on change projects

  o People directly impacted by the change

- o Cross-functional representation (representation from the business and not just from Human Resources)

- o Credibility within the organization

- o Members who were supportive and passionate about the change

- **Ensure budget and resources for change management**
  The change management effort and team must be resourced appropriately. This included allocating a budget for change management and providing dedicated resources.

- **Develop an effective relationship with the project team**
  While there were many variations on the suggested team structure, participants cited a structured and formal relationship with the project team. Some suggestions were to have all of the change management team on the project team, have a project team member on the change management team or create a liaison position. Participants also mentioned the importance of aligning objectives with the project team and integrating project management activities with change management.

- **Provide change management training**
  Change management training was suggested for the change management team and for project managers, senior leaders and front-line managers.

- **Understand the project details**
  The change management team should have a thorough understanding of the project itself to effectively create change management strategies and plans.

- **Start change management activities at the beginning of the project**
  Beginning change management activities at the start of a project enabled more proactive planning of change management efforts.

Source date: 2007

# Resources and budget

## Change management resources

Participants provided data on their change management budget and the change management resources (expressed as Full Time Equivalents or FTEs) working on their project.

The following tables and graphs show average change management FTEs and budget for various sized projects. Data is provided relative to project investment, number of employees impacted and scope of project.

The data showing average change management FTE on the project and average change management budget include only those participants who had dedicated change management resources on their team (responses of "0" were removed from the averages). About 6% of participants indicated "0" for change management FTE and 14% of participants indicated "0" for change management budget.

| Project investment | Avg FTE | Avg budget |
|---|---|---|
| $100K or less | 2.11 | $14,702 |
| $100K to $500K | 2.86 | $55,859 |
| $500K to $1M | 1.93 | $103,289 |
| $1M to $5M | 2.48 | $329,664 |
| $5M to $10M | 3.31 | $668,768 |
| More than $10M | 8.56 | $1,166,708 |

**Table 6 – Change management resources relative to project investment**

| Number of employees | Avg FTE | Avg budget |
|---|---|---|
| Less than 50 | 2.05 | $70,173 |
| 50 to 100 | 1.73 | $82,520 |
| 100 to 500 | 2.39 | $246,419 |
| 500 to 1000 | 3.67 | $287,842 |
| 1000 to 5000 | 4.38 | $685,967 |
| 5000 to 10,000 | 3.61 | $406,417 |
| 10K to 20K | 7.25 | $552,200 |
| More than 20K | 9.32 | $1,202,480 |

**Table 7 – Change management resources relative to number of employees impacted**

| Scope | Avg FTE | Avg budget |
|---|---|---|
| Within a workgroup | 0.85 | $18,333 |
| Single department | 2.27 | $41,038 |
| Multiple departments | 2.25 | $165,714 |
| Single division | 2.11 | $171,182 |
| Multiple divisions | 3.68 | $602,552 |
| Entire enterprise | 5.14 | $548,182 |

**Table 8 – Change management resources relative to scope of change**

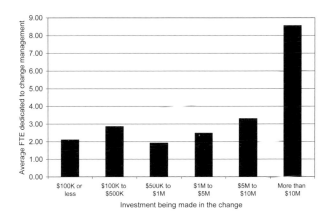

**Figure 11 – Change management FTE relative to project investment**

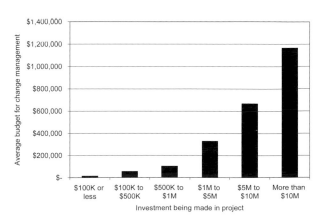

**Figure 12 – Change management budget relative to project investment**

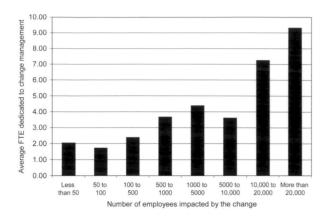

Figure 13 – Change management FTE
relative to number of employees impacted

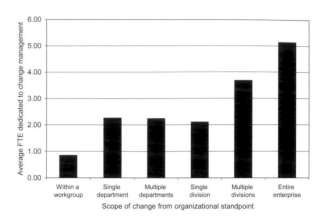

Figure 15 – Change management FTE
relative to scope

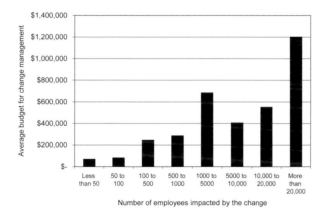

Figure 14 – Change management budget
relative to number of employees impacted

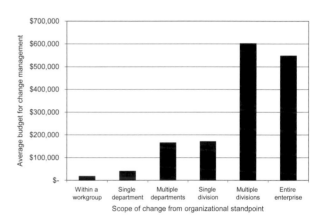

Figure 16 – Change management budget
relative to scope

## *Percentage of project FTE dedicated to change management*

Participants provided data on the Full Time Equivalents (FTEs) supporting the entire project and the FTEs dedicated to change management. Figure 17 shows a distribution of the percentage of project FTE that were dedicated to change management.

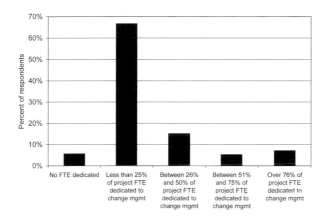

**Figure 17 – Change management FTE as percent of total project FTE**

Overall, the average percentage of project FTE dedicated to change management was 24%, paralleling the findings from the 2007 study. When those citing "0" change management FTE were removed, the average was 26%.

Participants also provided the appropriate or ideal FTE to assign to change management if this value was different than what they actually had. Nearly half of participants (47%) suggested a different change management staffing level. One third of participants suggested doubling the change management FTE. Participants, on average, recommended one-and-a-half times the number of change management FTE resources.

## *Change management budget*

As shown in Figure 18, over 60% of participants reported having too small of a change management budget, compared to 53% in the 2007 study.

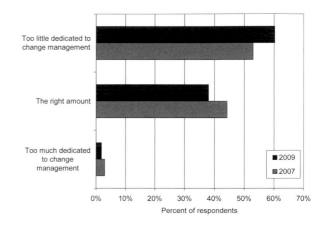

**Figure 18 – Change management budget**

# Sponsor role

## *Most important sponsor roles*

Study participants identified three critical roles for primary sponsors that are required for project success:

1. **Participate actively and visibly throughout the project**
   The role of active and visible participation for the primary sponsor was cited more frequently than any other sponsor activity. Study participants identified the following activities that characterize active and visible sponsorship:

   - Allocate the necessary resources and provide the necessary funding

   - Set expectations and establish clear objectives for the project

   - Hold the team accountable for results

   - Attend frequent project review meetings and actively review progress

   - Remove roadblocks and provide timely decisions on project issues

   - Be accessible to the project team; clear calendar when necessary to attend key events

   - Build support and enthusiasm for the change

   - Model the change through personal example and hands-on involvement

   - Provide unwavering support throughout the entire project

2. **Build a coalition of sponsorship and manage resistance**
   Participants stated the need for the primary sponsor to take a lead role in building the sponsorship coalition, including managing resistance from mid-level managers. Participants provided the following specific activities:

   - Build a strong sponsor coalition for the change among key business leaders and stakeholders

   - Determine and communicate priorities between this change and other change projects

   - Establish alignment around the overall business direction and the objectives of this change; resolve conflicting operational objectives with other senior leaders and middle management

   - Ensure that a consistent message about the change is being communicated by managers

   - Recognize outstanding managers and manage resistance from those managers not supporting the change with their employees; enforce consequences for non-compliance

   - Manage the expectations of stakeholders and customers

3. **Communicate directly with employees**
   Communications with employees, as cited by study participants, included the following:

   - Build awareness with employees about why the change is being made (what created the need for this change)

   - Share the risk or costs if no change is made (be open and honest with these communications)

   - Show how this change aligns with the overall direction of the organization

   - Share the goals and personal expectations for this project

   - Empathize with employees regarding the difficulties and additional work that will be required during the transition

   - Recognize the good work that employees have done and stress the positive benefits of the future state

- Celebrate successes with employees; be present and visible

- Listen to employees and encourage feedback; be willing to answer the tough questions

- Build excitement and enthusiasm around the change; show personal commitment

- Be willing to communicate to employees repeatedly to reinforce the message

Source date: 2007

## Most common mistakes made by executive sponsors

Study participants cited the biggest mistakes their primary sponsor made during their change projects:

1. **Failed to personally engage in the project**

    *"Was involved only at the beginning – announced the change and then walked away"*

    *"Did not conduct regular reviews; lacked frequent interactions with the project team"*

    *"Was invisible; did not participate and was not personally involved"*

    *"Assumed the change would happen without them; left the project on autopilot"*

2. **Avoided direct communications with employees**

    *"Did not share the vision and the rationale for the change with employees"*

    *"Lacked direct communications with supervisors and managers"*

    *"Did not deliver a consistent message"*

    *"Assumed that sharing things once was enough"*

3. **Abdicated or delegated his or her role as sponsor**

    *"Abdicated sponsorship to the project team and outside consultant"*

    *"Delegated their role; sponsor in name only"*

4. **Wavered in his or her support**

    *"Changed their position on the need for change; shifted direction mid-stream"*

    *"Moved on to other priorities; did not manage conflicting priorities"*

5. **Failed to build a coalition of sponsorship with key leaders in the organization**

    *"Lacked interaction with key stakeholders; did not listen and respond to their concerns"*

    *"Failed to set expectations with direct reports; assumed support would be there"*

Source date: 2007

## Understanding of roles

Figure 19 shows the participants' evaluation of how well their sponsors understood their roles and responsibilities. Consistent with the 2007 study, more than one half of participants reported that their sponsors had a less than adequate understanding of the role of an effective change leader.

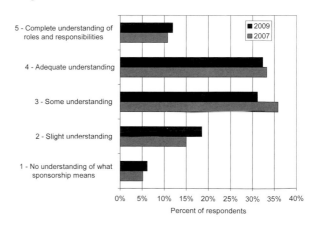

**Figure 19 – Sponsors' understanding of roles and responsibilities**

## Sponsor role challenges

Participants in the 2009 study were asked to evaluate how effective their sponsors were at fulfilling each of the three primary roles (see section "Most important sponsor roles").

Figure 20 shows the percentage of participants who indicated their sponsors were "ineffective" or "extremely ineffective" in fulfilling each role. One fifth of participants felt their sponsors were ineffective at being active and visible throughout the project, while nearly one third of participants indicated that their sponsors were not effectively communicating directly with employees.

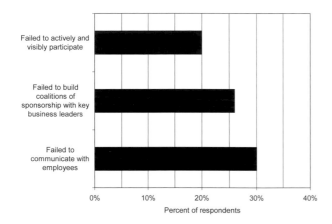

**Figure 20 – Percentage of participants that indicated ineffective or extremely ineffective sponsor role fulfillment**

## *Tactics for educating sponsors about their role*

Participants cited the most effective tactics to educate sponsors. Data from the 2007 and 2009 studies were combined to provide a number of tactics for educating sponsors about their role in change management, including:

1. **One-on-one meetings**
   In both the 2007 and 2009 studies, the number one recommendation for educating sponsors on their role in change management was through one-on-one discussions. Participants mentioned the need for these meetings to be face-to-face, open and regular. In many cases, participants would coach sponsors on a monthly or even weekly basis to further their understanding of what was required to be a successful sponsor. Sitting

down with the sponsor face-to-face provided an opportunity to connect and build a relationship. Specific recommendations from participants for this coaching included:

- **Create a roles and responsibilities document**
  This document clarified what was needed from the sponsor. Participants stated that providing the sponsor with an outline of specific requests and a timeline helped the sponsor complete the tasks necessary for project success.

  *"One-to-one discussion about what is expected of the sponsor, what he/she expects of you (the change manager or project manager), their current level of involvement, what actions they can take to be at the level of involvement you need them to be, and what support they need (from you and others) in order to get there."*

- **Keep the sponsor updated**
  Study participants listed regular meetings (weekly in most cases) to discuss project progress as a great way to educate the sponsor about their role. These meetings provided a forum to discuss issues and opportunities the project was facing, and to determine ways for the sponsor to actively facilitate success. The meetings also allowed the team to share sponsor feedback and improve future leadership.

- **Tie the sponsor role to project success**
  Participants wanted sponsors to understand how their role contributed to the success of the change, and the importance of having a "senior face" that provided open support for the project.

- **Explain the project details**
  By delving into the specifics of the project including objectives, desired outcomes and potential risks, the sponsor was able to appreciate the significance of the change.

2. **Change management training**
Many participants found that formalized training provided the sponsor with a greater understanding of change management as a whole, as well as their role as a leader during change. Providing sponsors with tools and articles to further their learning also contributed to success. Training enabled sponsors to answer key questions like:

- Why change management?

- What are the financial benefits of change management and consequences for not doing change management?

  *"Define cost/benefit associated with the effective management of change, develop their understanding of the risks associated with not doing [change management] and quote specific examples."*

- Is the sponsor role critical to success?

3. **Provide communications support**
Participants found that when they needed the sponsor to share a particular message with employees, the sponsor fulfilled this role more effectively when the project team or change manager provided the vehicles and communication packages in completed form. By having the team "ghost write" the messages, the sponsor was able to devote more time to effective communications.

## *Engaging reluctant senior leaders*

Participants cited the most effective techniques to engage resistant or reluctant senior leaders. Results from both the 2007 and 2009 studies are combined below to provide a more complete set of recommendations from study participants:

1. **Clearly demonstrate the benefits of the change and the risks of not changing**
Participants stated that benefits of the change should be communicated in language meaningful to that senior leader – "speak their language." The business case should be clearly presented with a focus on the business outcomes and how the change aligns with the business strategy, as well as the risks to the

business if this change is not made. Use financials and hard data, and include the results from early trials when available. These discussions should also include how the change will impact them and the "WIIFM" (What's in it for me?). Where possible, align the change with their goals.

2. **Direct intervention by the primary sponsor**
Participants cited the need for direct intervention of the primary sponsor to manage resistance from other senior leaders. Participants indicated that the primary sponsor should:

- Ensure alignment around the business strategy and associated changes

- Set priorities and clearly communicate his or her expectations of each senior leader

- Build an effective leadership coalition

- Adjust the compensation and evaluation system to align with the change

- Implement consequences for those unwilling to support the change

3. **Increase the level of involvement of resistant senior leaders**
Participants suggested increasing the level of involvement and decision making of resistant senior leaders, including scheduling more frequent meetings, engaging them earlier in the process and gathering input from them on key design decisions. Participants indicated that senior leaders should be involved in the planning process up front and should have ownership in the final solution for changes impacting their area.

4. **Identify the root cause of the resistance**
Participants cited the need to clearly identify the root cause of the resistance by listening to the specific objections of senior leaders. Participants indicated that it was important to understand why the resistance was occurring and to explore the reasons in depth.

5. **Increase the level of one-on-one interactions**
Participants stated that one-on-one

interactions were essential to manage resistance from senior leaders. Participants encouraged face-to-face conversations that were candid and frequent.

6. **Provide coaching on their role as a sponsor**
Many senior leaders were new to change management and needed more clearly defined responsibilities. Participants found it effective to coach them on their role, what it meant and how they were key to the success of the project. Special tactics such as developing a specific roadmap of activities or preparing communication messages were mentioned.

7. **Provide project details**
Many "important" projects came across the desks of senior leaders each day, so it was critical that they truly understood the meaning of the project they were being asked to support. Study participants said they engaged senior leaders by providing clear project details, benefits of the project (impact on the bottom line, meeting target audience needs) and risks of project failure.

8. **Regular communications**
Continued engagement of senior leaders was maintained through ongoing communications. Creating an open, one-on-one channel was a key success factor. Participants also found success in keeping senior leaders informed on progress through daily reports or updates on the status of risks and issues.

## How would you characterize your sponsor at the beginning of the project?

The 2009 study included a new question about how participants would characterize their sponsors at the beginning of the project (Figure 21). Nearly three quarters of participants characterized their sponsors positively at the beginning of the project – with 34% indicating sponsors were proactive and enthusiastic, and 39% indicating sponsors were willing and ready to do what was asked of them. Only 4% of study

participants stated their sponsors were extremely resistant and unwilling to be a sponsor of change.

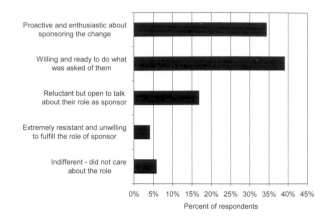

**Figure 21 – Sponsor characterization at beginning of the project**

## Sponsor access

Participants indicated their level of access to the sponsor. Over one third of participants indicted that they had inadequate or no access to sponsors throughout the project (Figure 22).

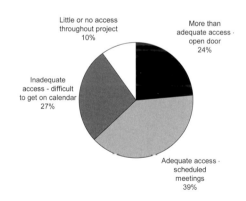

**Figure 22 – Access to sponsor**

In addition to overall sponsor access, participants indicated how frequently they met with sponsors during the project (Figure 23). Over half of participants reported meeting only monthly or quarterly with their sponsors. Conversely, over half of participants indicated that they would prefer weekly meetings with their sponsor.

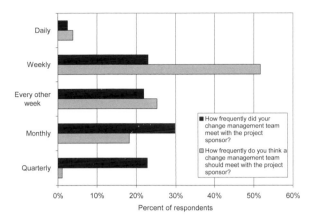

**Figure 23 – Frequency of meeting with sponsors - actual and desired**

## Sponsor communication frequency

Study participants identified how many times per month their sponsor communicated to employees about a particular change. Figure 24 shows the data for direct communication frequency. Over one half of participants said that their sponsor communicated directly with employees only once per month or less.

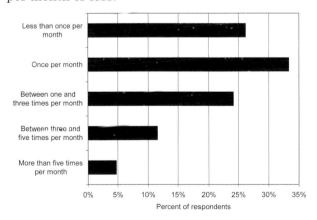

**Figure 24 – Sponsor communication frequency**

## Consequences of sponsorship at the wrong level

Participants who had sponsors at the wrong level struggled with their projects, citing many severe consequences to the change and to the organization, including:

- Delayed projects – *"we are behind schedule"*

- Failed changes – *"we were not able to complete the change"*

- Frustrated and resistant employees – *"people are ignoring the change"* or *"key stakeholders are not engaged"*

- Difficulty acquiring resources and funding

- Missed project objectives or project objectives that kept changing

- Slow decision making or the inability to make decisions

Editor's note: When asked about tactics to secure the right level of sponsorship, participants provided a wide range of possible solutions. Some ideas included: do the project anyway (work under the radar), find a substitute sponsor, skip levels and go above the manager who would not sponsor the project or integrate the change with another project that does have a sponsor. Past research has suggested the following two options: 1) identify the correct sponsor(s) for the change and solicit their support and engagement as the primary sponsor (clearly present the business case and risks of not changing) or 2) scale back the change to match the sponsorship that is available. Choosing to proceed with the change without the necessary sponsorship typically results in the consequences cited here.

Source date: 2007

---

# Sponsor activities

Participants described the most important sponsor activities for managing change. The data was broken into three major project phases: start-up (planning), design and implementation. The activities and steps were further categorized by the primary target audiences:

- Project team
- Managers and business leaders (executive and senior management)
- Employees

Figure 25 below is a 3 x 3 diagram illustrating the responsibilities of the sponsor in each project phase (start-up, design, and implementation). The activities required for each box in this figure are described in detail on the following pages.

Note: The labels for each box in Figure 25 are intended to be general descriptions for the category and are not intended to stand alone from the activity lists in Tables 9, 10 and 11.

Editor's note: The Sponsor Responsibilities Model shown below was first developed in 2003. This model includes data from the 2003, 2005 and 2007 studies.

Source date: 2007

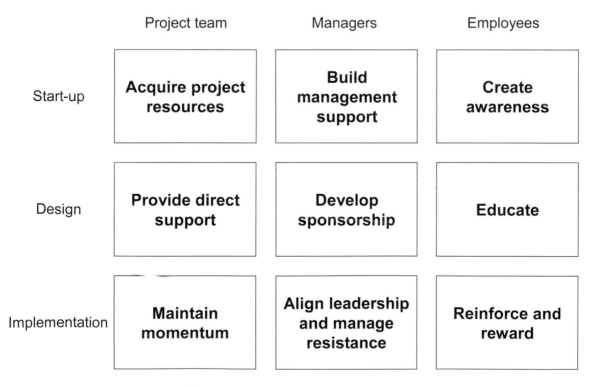

**Figure 25 – Sponsor Responsibilities Model**

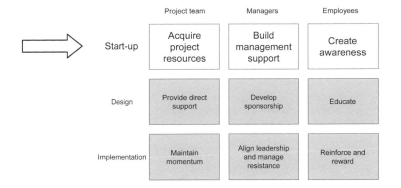

| | with the Project team | with Managers | with Employees |
|---|---|---|---|
| | **Acquire project resources** | **Build management support** | **Create awareness** |
| **Start-up** | • Select the best project leader and team members; include resources with change management expertise<br><br>• Provide necessary funding for the team, including training for all team members on change management<br><br>• Set priorities related to day-to-day work vs. project work to allow adequate team member participation<br><br>• Help the team understand the critical business issues or opportunities that must be addressed<br><br>• Provide clear direction and objectives for the project; describe what success will look like<br><br>• Jointly develop a high-level view of the future and link the change to the business strategy<br><br>• Be directly involved with the project team; set expectations; review key deliverables and remove obstacles<br><br>• Take ownership for success of the project and hold the team accountable for results | • Enlist the support of executive managers and create a support network (coalition of managers needed to support the change)<br><br>• Create a steering committee of key managers to monitor progress (dependent on project size)<br><br>• Educate senior managers about the business drivers for change and the risks of not changing<br><br>• Work directly with managers who show early signs of resistance<br><br>• Create change advocates within the leadership team; build support and enthusiasm for the change<br><br>• Provide training on change management for senior managers<br><br>• Establish change activities that the leadership group is responsible for completing<br><br>• Define accountabilities for mid-level managers<br><br>• Determine and communicate priorities between this change and other change initiatives<br><br>• Resolve conflicting operational objectives with other senior leaders | • Describe the current state of the business and share the business issues or opportunities<br><br>• Explain why a change is needed now; share the risks of not changing<br><br>• Share a vision for the future; explain the nature of the change and show how the change will address the business problems or opportunities<br><br>• Answer the questions: "How will this change affect me?" and "What's in it for me?"<br><br>• Be proactive, vocal and visible; communicate frequently, including face-to-face<br><br>• Listen and be open to dialogue and resistance<br><br>• Tell employees what they can expect to happen and when<br><br>• Understand the organizational culture and beliefs<br><br>• Repeat key messages over and over<br><br>• Share plans with customers and suppliers<br><br>• Show project milestones and provide progress updates |

**Table 9 – Sponsor start-up activities**

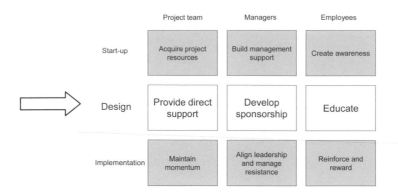

| | with the Project team | with Managers | with Employees |
|---|---|---|---|
| **Design** | **Provide direct support** | **Develop sponsorship** | **Educate** |
| | • Stay involved: attend key project meetings, review project status and hold the team accountable for results<br>• Provide the necessary resources and funding, including ensuring that the right people are made available to support the design work<br>• Be accessible to the team; be a sounding board; provide ideas and constructive criticism to the team; ask "What if?"<br>• Remove roadblocks; make timely decisions on project issues and help manage conflicts and political issues<br>• Communicate expectations and feedback from other managers<br>• Keep the team on track and manage "scope creep"<br>• Reward success stories and achievements<br>• Take the time to understand the solution<br>• Identify conflicts with other projects that may impact this team<br>• Make sure the project team knows that your door is open and you are available to support their work | • Continue to build support and sponsorship among senior managers; reinforce the key messages; resolve differences in perception; address areas of resistance<br>• Let senior managers know how they can proactively support the change; provide them with a clear roadmap for sponsoring the change with their direct reports<br>• Conduct steering committee meetings; keep managers informed; use this forum to resolve critical issues<br>• Use public and private conversations to reinforce leadership support; recognize outstanding managers<br>• Communicate project progress to all executive managers<br>• Hold mid-level managers accountable<br>• Do not tolerate resistance from mid-level managers or allow managers to "opt out" of the change; be clear on expectations<br>• Ensure that a consistent message is being sent by managers to impacted employees | • Communicate frequently with employees; make your personal commitment visible, including face-to-face conversations<br>• Reinforce the reason for change, the risk of not changing and the evolving details about the future state<br>• Show employees how the change aligns with the direction and strategy for the business<br>• Answer the question "What will this change mean to me?"<br>• Listen to what employees have to say; take the pulse of the organization and collect feedback<br>• Share project progress and provide updates on a regular basis; update employees on "what you can expect to happen and when"<br>• Enable employee participation and involvement<br>• Recognize the good work that employees have done<br>• Involve customers and suppliers |

**Table 10 – Sponsor design activities**

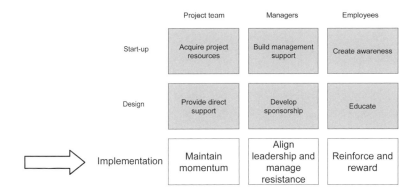

| | with the Project team | with Managers | with Employees |
|---|---|---|---|
| **Implementation** | **Maintain momentum** | **Align leadership and manage resistance** | **Reinforce and reward** |
| | • Secure resources necessary for implementation<br><br>• Stay engaged with the team: attend meetings, reward successes, hold them accountable for results and build enthusiasm<br><br>• Remove roadblocks and help the team overcome obstacles<br><br>• Stay the course; avoid shifting priorities too early | • Continue to meet in public and private with business leaders and senior managers; align sponsorship; provide progress updates; resolve issues<br><br>• Communicate expectations to senior managers for their support of the change; provide activities they can do and messages they can communicate to their organizations<br><br>• Manage resistance from middle managers; correct or remove managers who will not support the change<br><br>• Model the change through personal example and hands-on involvement<br><br>• Stay involved throughout the entire project; stay visible | • Reinforce key messages; align business strategy with project objectives; increase personal communications<br><br>• Reinforce why the change is being made and the risk of not changing (some employees may be ready to hear this message only when the change is near implementation)<br><br>• Listen to employees and encourage feedback; be willing to answer the tough questions<br><br>• Set expectations for employees; clearly communicate consequences of not changing<br><br>• Identify with the additional work and difficulties that may be experienced during implementation<br><br>• Enforce application of new processes and behaviors<br><br>• Look for quick wins; share successes and build enthusiasm for the change<br><br>• Celebrate success stories; be present and visible |

**Table 11 – Sponsor implementation activities**

# Managers and supervisors

## *Importance of manager and supervisor involvement*

Participants ranked how important they felt manager and supervisor involvement was to the success of a change effort (Figure 26). The results were quite clear, with 84% of participants ranking manager and supervisor involvement as extremely or very important. Only 4% of participants indicated that involvement was somewhat important or not important.

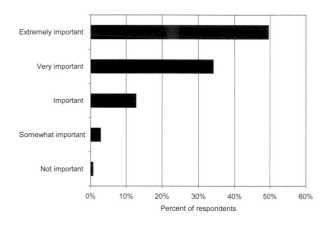

**Figure 26 – Importance of manager and supervisor involvement in success of change effort**

## *Roles of managers and supervisors in times of change*

Participants were asked to identify the most critical roles that managers and supervisors should play when introducing change into the organization. The top five responses were:

1. **Communicate with direct reports about the change**
   Managers and supervisors should explain why the change is needed and link the change to the employee's job role. Managers and supervisors should provide details about the change and discuss the impact on employees. Additionally, managers should create a dialogue by listening to employees, gathering feedback and answering questions.

2. **Demonstrate support for the change**
   Managers and supervisors should actively demonstrate their support and enthusiasm for the change. They must become true advocates and promote the change with their direct reports (be a role model).

3. **Coach employees through the change process**
   Managers and supervisors should support their employees throughout the transition and act as coaches for direct reports. These actions serve to maintain and build trust with impacted employees. Participants also cited leadership, motivation and mentoring on the part of supervisors as keys to effective coaching.

4. **Engage with and provide support to the project team**
   Managers and supervisors should provide feedback to the project team, acting as a liaison between impacted employees and the groups directing the change. They should provide data on how well employees are embracing the change, as well as any performance issues.

5. **Identify and manage resistance**
   Given their close proximity to front-line employees, managers and supervisors should identify and manage resistance to the change with their direct reports.

Participants also stated that to fulfill the roles outlined above, managers and supervisors needed a foundational understanding of both the change itself and their role in change management.

Source date: 2007

## Manager role challenges

Figure 27 shows the percentage of participants who indicated that their managers and supervisors were "ineffective" or "extremely ineffective" at a particular role. The two roles that managers and supervisors struggled with most were coaching employees through the change process, and identifying and managing resistance.

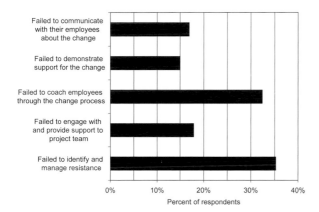

**Figure 27 – Percentage of participants indicating ineffective or extremely ineffective manager role fulfillment**

## Most common mistakes made by managers and supervisors

The top three most common mistakes made by managers and supervisors during change were:

1. **Not effectively communicating with their employees**
   By a large margin, the biggest mistake made by managers was failure to communicate effectively. Participants cited a number of symptoms of poor communications, including communications that were poorly timed, inaccurate, late, not targeted to the audience or that failed to explain why the change was happening. Additionally, managers made the mistake of "telling" rather than creating two-way communications. Some managers were also criticized for holding back pertinent information.

2. **Actively resisting the change**
   Participants indicated that some managers and supervisors actively resisted the change. Some managers joined the rumor mill distributing misinformation, while others created an "us vs. them" split between their direct group and the project.

3. **Ignoring the change**
   Some managers did not actively resist the change, but did not visibly support the change either. By ignoring the change, managers sent a message to their employees that this change was not important.

Additional mistakes cited by study participants included:

- Failure to involve employees
- Ignoring concerns from employees or treating their concerns as unimportant
- Not listening to employees or acknowledging feedback
- Failure to consider the impact of the change on individuals
- Ignoring resistance
- Viewing communications and their role as a one-time event

Source date: 2007

## Tactics for gaining support from managers

Participants identified the tactics they used to gain support and engage with managers and supervisors. The most frequently cited tactics included:

1. **Involving managers and supervisors in the project**
   Managers and supervisors were engaged in project planning and solution design. This allowed them to have a voice and to take ownership in project success. Involvement occurred through two-way communications, focus groups, input on scheduling and assessments, and consultation on key decisions.

2. **Highlighting the benefits of the change**
   Creating awareness about the benefits of the future state, both for the individual managers and for their teams, occurred by showing measurable outcomes such as cost savings and return on investment, as well as by answering the questions: "what's in it for me?", "what's in it for my team?" and "what's in it for the customers?".

3. **Maintaining frequent and honest communications**
   Managers were kept "in the loop" through ongoing communications that were open and honest. Status reports were provided frequently (bi-weekly, weekly or twice per week basis).

4. **Demonstrating active sponsorship**
   Participants leveraged project sponsors to gain support for the change among managers and supervisors. Both executive sponsors and middle managers demonstrated visible and clear support for the change by providing funding, facilitating meetings and being available to answer questions. Sponsorship provided accountability and helped to set priorities.

5. **Delivering training and workshops**
   Participants provided training and best practices information to managers that addressed skills, strategies and tools for leading change.

6. **Providing opportunities to voice resistance**
   Managers and supervisors were provided with opportunities to express their opinions and concerns to their supervisors and the change team. Participants listened carefully to understand the feedback and then took appropriate action to address concerns.

Other successful tactics for building support and engagement among managers included:

- Having one-on-one interaction

- Building open, transparent relationships

- Linking deliverables to performance objectives for accountability

- Building managers awareness of their critical role in successful change

- Giving managers a role in communicating project information to their teams

- Providing a formal support network

- Reinforcing successes through rewards and celebrations

- Connecting the change to organizational goals and values

## How to support managers and supervisors during change

Study participants offered a variety of suggestions on how to support managers and supervisors during change:

1. Designate a change champion or change team to coach and mentor managers. These subject matter experts could provide expertise and moral support while working through issues with managers. Some organizations established a helpdesk to put managers in touch with resources quickly.

2. Engage in constant dialogue and daily face-to-face communications with managers.

3. Provide tools for managers and supervisors to use while rolling out the change including: media kits, job aides, talking points, communication scripts, change management articles, case studies, reference materials and FAQs.

4. Collect information related to the change from employees via electronic or paper surveys, and share the feedback with managers and supervisors.

5. Share progress updates (keep managers and supervisors up-to-date and recognize when milestones have been achieved).

Other tactics to support managers and supervisors included:

- Offering formal change management training

- Creating awareness for change amongst all departments

- Conducting process/technology training
- Setting goals

## Formal change management training for managers

Forty percent of participants in the 2009 study provided formal change management training to managers and supervisors, compared to 39% in the 2007 study (Figure 28).

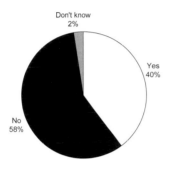

**Figure 28 – Provided formal change management training to managers**

Figure 29 shows how much time these study participants devoted to training managers on change management. More than one half of participants devoted one to three days of training time for their managers.

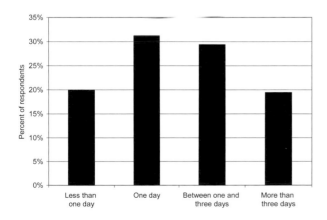

**Figure 29 – Duration of manager and supervisor change management training**

## Additional training methods

In addition to formal classroom training, participants offered the following approaches for building change management skills and knowledge with managers and supervisors:

- **One-on-one discussions and coaching**
  These sessions provided safe interactions to help managers and supervisors lead change with their direct reports. Participants mentioned peer coaching, mentoring by senior leaders and support from change management specialists as useful skill-building methods.

- **Formal, regular communications**
  These one-to-many communications included emails, pamphlets, newsletters, bulletin boards and electronic forum messages.

- **Meetings**
  In some cases change management was added as an agenda item to normal meetings. Meetings focusing on change management specifically included short presentations, road shows, "lunch and learn" opportunities and forums covering a particular change management issue.

- **Workshops and seminars**
  The most effective sessions were interactive and included problem solving, question-and-answer facilitation and role playing.

- **Tools**
  Managers and supervisors were provided tip sheets, quick reference guides, workbooks and toolkits to support their change management efforts.

- **Articles and books**
  Managers and supervisors were provided with additional literature on leading change.

The content addressed in these additional training methods included:

- Specific roles and responsibilities of the manager or supervisor to support the change management effort

- Project-related information including details of the project plan, business case, key messages for communications and progress updates

- Stories and experiences including success stories from previous changes and examples of issues or concerns from the current change

## Most important skills and tools needed by managers and supervisors

Study participants identified the most important change management skills and tools needed by managers and supervisors. These included:

- **Communication skills**
  How to facilitate effective two-way communications, hold question-and-answer sessions, and translate messages so they are meaningful to the audience

- **Techniques for managing resistance**
  How to identify and manage resistance along with approaches for surfacing employee concerns

- **Leadership skills**
  How to lead people through change; including interpersonal and motivational skills

- **Understanding of the human reaction to change**
  How to manage their employees as unique individuals going through a transition (specifically how to deal with the human reaction to change)

- **General change management knowledge**

- **Tools for measuring outcomes**

Participants also stated that managers should be provided with:

- An understanding of the change (what is changing, impacts of the change, why the change is happening and current status)

- Project-specific messages to communicate to employees, such as information packets, talking points and prepared question-and-answer information on the details of the particular change

Source date: 2007

## Evaluating manager and supervisor change management effectiveness

More than 80% of all study participants evaluated the effectiveness of managers and supervisors in fulfilling their change management roles. The methods used to evaluate the managers' change management skill level varied from informal and casual in nature to a formalized process to gather the data and appraise the effectiveness. The methods cited, in order of frequency, were:

- Employee surveys (specifically surveys assessing employee understanding of change messages communicated by their managers, as well as employee perceptions of the change overall)

- Informal face-to-face conversations with employees (to gain a sense of employee attitudes and their understanding of the change underway)

- Observations by change management team members (change management team members could join team meetings and listen to managers present the change to employees, thereby directly assessing the managers' ability to influence their employees and manage the change)

- Successful implementation of the business change

  *"Adoption of [the] new process was our measure for success."*

- Utilization of a formalized change management assessment tool implemented at periodic intervals throughout the life of the project

# Communications

## Attributes of a successful change message

Participants identified three attributes of a successful change message when communicating to employees:

1. **Shares what the change will mean to the employee**
   Employees want to hear about how the change will impact them personally, including:

   - How will this change impact me?

   - What will I do differently?

   - What's in it for me? (WIIFM)

   Employees want to know how the change will affect their job, including the impact on day-to-day job duties, reporting responsibilities and changes in compensation.

2. **Explains the business reasons for why the change is happening**
   Employees want to know why the change is important and necessary for the success of the business, as well as the specific benefits to the business as a whole. Employees need to understand the business reasons for the change and how the change aligns with the organization's goals, vision and strategy. Employees also want to know what would happen to the business if the change was not made (essentially, the consequence of inaction).

3. **Is honest and clear**
   Employees want to hear a message that is sincere, truthful and accurate. The message should include the good and the bad as well as honest answers about what the communicator does and does not know.

   *"Say what you know and admit what you don't know."*

Additional components of an effective change message from the 2007 Best Practices report include:

- **Shares what is changing**
  The message should define the overall nature of the change and what specifically is changing in the organization. Information about the transition from the current state to the future state, and what is expected of the employees during this transition period, should also be included.

- **Conveys the impact on the organization**
  Employees should know how the organization and specific departments will be affected by the change, as well as any benefits or negative impacts that may result.

- **Prepares employees for the change**
  Employees should be assured they are not alone when moving into the future state. They should have a clear picture of the training and support they will receive to enable them to make the transition. This may include help desks, ongoing training or online resources.

## Attributes of successful communicators

In addition to commenting on effective messages, participants in the 2009 study also shared feedback on effective communicators. The most successful and effective communicators demonstrated the following ten attributes, in rank order:

1. **Committed, engaged and passionate about the change**
   Successful communicators were positive, enthusiastic and passionate about the change – they believed in it. They were committed and engaged in the change and showed their support actively and visibly. They were champions of the change and led by example.

2. **Credible**
   Effective communicators were trusted and respected, and had the ability to influence all levels in the organization. They had experience and authority.

3. **Able to deliver a clear message**
Delivering a clear message meant one that was simple, focused and concise. Effective and successful communicators were able to deliver clear messages in non-technical language that could be understood by all receivers.

4. **Knowledgeable about the change and its impact on the organization**
Successful communicators understood why the change was needed, the purpose and benefits of the change, and its impacts on the people. They were also knowledgeable about the organization, internal processes and the organization's history. They connected this knowledge with their ability to see the "big picture" vision and future state. Their communications shared this perspective and context.

*"Explained clearly the organizational reason for the change and the personal impact on the individual; did this in an informative and respectful way."*

5. **Consistent and timely in their messages**
Communicators delivered frequent messages on a regular schedule. These messages remained consistent and were repeated often.

6. **Open and honest**
Open and honest meant the communicators and their messages were genuine and delivered with truth and transparency.

7. **Two-way communicators**
The most important element for communicators in two-way communications was the ability to listen. Two-way communicators were open to conversations and feedback.

8. **Fluent in the "language" of their audience**
Effective communicators created a message that was tailored and relevant to their receivers. They always included the answer to, "What's in it for me?" for the intended audience.
*"Taking the broad message and making it meaningful for the group being communicated with."*

9. **Personable**
Personable communicators were patient, confident and compassionate. They had excellent interpersonal skills, communicated with empathy and were approachable.

10. **Choosing the right channel**
Choosing the right channel meant the ability to offer communications in a variety of ways while ensuring that face-to-face communications was one of those channels.

## Most effective communication methods

According to study participants, face-to-face methods of communicating with employees about change were the most effective, and included:

1. **Group meetings and presentations**
Participants recommended group meetings that included the opportunity for feedback and interaction between managers and employees. Question-and-answer sessions allowed for additional interaction and clarification. Examples included forums, town hall meetings, small group meetings, large group presentations, focus groups, workshops and seminars.

*"Presentations are a good way to communicate because that's the best way to make sure all participants have the understanding and their questions have been answered."*

2. **One-on-one coaching sessions and discussions**
Participants recommended one-on-one sessions to address individual concerns and points of resistance among employees. These one-on-one sessions created an environment of trust, honesty and safety and enabled the communicator to genuinely listen to and answer employee concerns. Examples included individual coaching meetings, informal personal conversations or walk-arounds and the use of "champions" within a group or department.

*"One-on-one discussions, although more time-consuming, allow full discussion of proposals and understanding on both sides."*

Participants also commented on the prudent use of non-personal, electronic or written feedback mechanisms as a way to allow employees to ask questions and provide feedback through alternative channels. Suggestions included:

- Electronic messaging system

- Employee surveys and quick polls

- Web boards or online forums

- Notice boards with comment cards throughout departments

- Suggestion box by email or voicemail

Source date: 2007

## *Preferred senders of change messages*

Participants in the 2007 study cited two preferred senders of change messages (Figure 30) mirroring the findings of the 2005 and 2003 benchmarking studies.

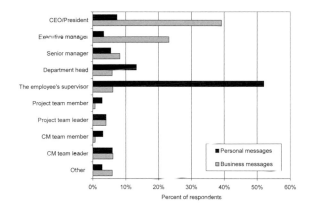

**Figure 30 – Preferred senders of change messages**

For business messages related to the change, such as how the change aligns with the organization's strategy, why the change is being made and the risk of not changing, employees want to hear from a senior business leader (the person in charge). For messages related to the personal implications of the change, including how the change will impact their job role and

"What's in it for me?" or WIIFM, employees prefer to hear from their immediate supervisor.

Source date: 2007

## *Additional messages for managers and supervisors*

In addition to the important messages to be communicated to all employees, participants in the study cited the following essential points that must be communicated to managers and supervisors:

- **Their role in the change process and the importance of their involvement**
  Managers and supervisors must understand their role as change agents, leaders and coaches to their employees during the change process. Clearly explain their responsibilities and the critical need for their buy-in and leadership. Encourage them to "lead by example" with employees.

- **How to support their employees through change**
  Empower managers and supervisors with tools to manage change with their employees, including how to communicate the change message, strategies for dealing with resistance and progress updates on the change project so they can pass information along to their staff. Also, offer additional ongoing support for issues that may arise or questions they may have.

Source date: 2007

## *Tactics for correcting misinformation and misunderstandings*

There were six different tactics used for correcting misunderstandings resulting from background conversations or the "rumor mill":

1. **Enabling open discussion time**
   Open discussion time included events that allowed people to exchange information freely, present questions and provide feedback. Open discussions happened in many different formats including: town halls,

brown bag lunches, road show presentations, conference calls, site visits, forums, small group meetings and focus groups.

2. **Identifying current rumors and addressing them immediately**
It was important that the identification of current rumors be done anonymously. Participants cited the following ways to collect rumors anonymously: telephone hotlines, designated email addresses, help desks and collection boxes. Participants also noted that it was best to address those rumors, when possible, in a face-to-face format.

3. **Engaging sponsors**
Participants cited many different methods of engaging leadership. No matter how sponsors were engaged, sponsors were recognized as the most effective group to address and correct background conversations resulting from misinformation.

*"National leadership team traveled to each location and allowed an opportunity for Q&A."*

4. **Providing regular communications**
Regular communications were a source of consistency and provided updated information on the change. The most common interval of regular communications among participants was weekly, followed by monthly.

5. **Updating "Frequently Asked Questions"**
Frequently Asked Questions (FAQs) answered common questions and addressed misinformation spreading through background conversations. FAQs were updated on a regular basis and circulated among employees in various ways including newsletters, electronic postings and written documentation.

6. **Providing electronic sources of information**
A source of information that could be accessed electronically at any time by employees and could be updated by the team was a useful tool for keeping employees up-to-date. This source of information was available to everyone in the organization to provide a sense of transparency and openness. Participants also cited the value of interactions through an electronic source including blogs, discussion boards and postings.

*"Set up a 'rumor busters' website and fed it with both real and manufactured rumors and corrections."*

## What to do differently next time

When asked how they would change their communications approach for the next project, participants cited a number of changes they would make. Consistent with previous studies, the most common response was to communicate more often. The top five responses included:

1. **Communicate more often**
Increase the frequency of messages to ensure they are understood and reinforced.

2. **Engage managers and supervisors more effectively as communicators**
Involve managers and supervisors more as the senders of messages to employees and empower them with information to be effective champions of change.

*"Make sure that the supervisors are champions for change – and championing the right messages; this group can be both the most positive and negative influencers of change communication."*

3. **Make the communications plan a formal project deliverable with appropriate staffing and resources**
Write a formal communications plan early in the planning stage and assign dedicated staff members to manage and execute the plan.

*"Attempt to lay out an overall communication approach that integrates the project and change process together."*

4. **Start communicating with employees earlier in the project**
Proactively communicate with employees as details of the change project emerge to prevent rumors or early resistance to the change.

*"Start communicating as soon as the need for change is recognized."*

5. **Use more communication methods and channels**
Understand all communication channels available and their value; incorporate additional methods to reach employees in unique and effective ways

Source date: 2007


## *Frequency of communications*

Overall, participants tended to communicate less frequently than what they considered to be ideal. The largest gap appeared in the "less than monthly" category where over 12% of participants fell, but less than 2% felt was ideal. The majority of participants suggested a communication frequency in the range of several times a week to monthly, with about one third stating that weekly was the ideal frequency of communications (Figure 31).

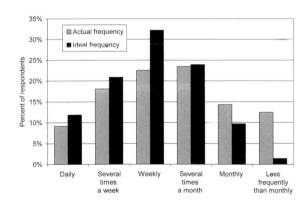

## **Figure 31 – Communications frequency**

Source date: 2007

## Complete listing of communication methods

Participants used a variety of communication methods during their change projects. In total, over 200 different methods were used to communicate change. Although the most effective communication methods were cited earlier, the list below is included to help change management teams brainstorm additional communication methods. This list includes input from participants in the 2003, 2005 and 2007 benchmarking studies:

- Articles in industry journals
- Banners
- Billboards
- Blogs
- Booklets
- Briefings
- Brochures
- Brown bag lunches
- Bulletins
- Bulletin boards
- Café meetings
- Cafeteria postings
- Cascading communication trees
- Charts/graphs to show progress
- Circulars
- Coffee mornings
- Demonstrations
- Desk drops
- Electronic billboards/plasma screens
- Email
- Fact sheets
- Faxes
- Fliers
- Frequently Asked Questions (FAQs)
- Focus groups
- Gallery walks
- Giveaways
- Group meetings
- Hallway conversations
- Industrial theater
- Information fairs
- Intranet pop-ups
- Internal messaging system
- Leaflets

- Lectures
- Letters
- Lunch and learns
- Mailers
- Memos
- Newsletters (corporate and project)
- One-on-one meetings and coaching
- Pamphlets
- Pay stub inserts
- Posters
- Presentations
- Project fairs
- Public celebrations
- Rallies
- Recognition packages
- Reader boards
- Road shows
- Roundtables
- Site visits
- Skits
- Status reports
- Storyboards
- Success stories
- Surveys
- Team meetings
- Teleconferences
- Testimonials
- Text messages
- Town hall meetings
- Tradeshows
- Training courses
- TVs
- Videos
- Voicemail messages
- Walk-arounds
- Webcasts
- Webinars
- Website (Intranet)
- Word of mouth
- Workshops

Source date: 2007

# Training

The 2009 study included questions related to training for employees on the new processes, skills and behaviors required by the project, as well as the role the change management team played in project-related training.

## *Primary methods used to train employees*

The top five methods used to train employees on the new processes, skills and behaviors required by the change were:

- Classroom training (nearly half of all study participants utilized classroom education to train their employees on the new skills required)

- One-on-one coaching or mentoring

- Self-paced, web-based training

- Hands-on training (gave employees an opportunity to try the tools and have support available for immediate feedback)

- Job aides (hard copy aides for the new tools and processes including reference cards, user manuals, FAQs or cheat sheets)

Participants shared the following insights related to the most effective training techniques:

- Hands-on training was overwhelmingly the most effective training method. Participants found it to be the most beneficial because there was an opportunity to try out the new system in a safe environment and receive immediate feedback. Some examples of hands-on training included live demonstrations, role plays and simulations.

- One-on-one coaching was an important element of the participants' training efforts. During the coaching sessions, managers were able to answer the employees' questions as well as assess their ability to use the new tool.

- While classroom-style training was found to be beneficial to address large groups, small group discussions were also utilized as a training technique. The small group setting allowed for open discussions and addressed the "what" and "why" as well as what was in it for the employee.

Follow-up support was an important element of training to aide in reinforcement. It was also beneficial to assess the comfort level of the employees with the new processes.

## *Role of change management team*

The role the change management team played in project-related training included:

- **The creation, planning and delivery of training**
  Sixty-two percent of all study participants said their change management team planned, created and delivered the training.

  *"Change management led the entire training effort, from development to leading sessions."*

- **To support, coach and oversee the training**
  The change management team's role was to support and oversee the training program. Change managers were responsible for "providing ongoing consultation and support to the trainers."

- **Communications**
  Change managers were responsible for communicating the when, what and how related to the project training as well as ensuring key messages were present during the training program.

# Resistance

### *Primary reasons employees resisted change*

Data from Prosci's 2007 and 2009 reports reveal consistent themes for why employees resisted change. Specifically, participants cited five top reasons that front-line employees resisted change in their organizations, including:

1. **Lack of awareness**
   Employees resisted change because they lacked awareness of why the change was being made or did not understand the nature of the change. They did not know the business reasons for making a change or the consequences of not changing. Study participants stated that employees resisted more when they did not have the answer to the question "what's in it for me?" or WIIFM. Participants also said that employees lacked awareness because their managers were uninformed or were sending mixed messages.

2. **Impact on current job role**
   Many employees resisted change when they believed there would be a negative impact on their job role or workload. Specifically, employees were resistant to changes that:

   - Increased the amount of work they would be required to perform (too busy already)

   - Did not allow for current process "work-arounds"

   - Would cause a loss of position or power when the change was implemented (employees feared that the change and the associated performance measures would "work against them")

3. **Organization's past performance with change**
   Employees cited the organization's past failure to implement changes as a factor in their lack of commitment to a current change. Some participants cited a culture of non-compliance or "serial resistors" as factors contributing to employee resistance. Many

participants also stated that front-line employees were resistant to any type of change because these employees were comfortable or "entrenched" in the old way of doing things.

4. **Lack of visible support and commitment from managers**
   Participants cited a lack of support from employees when the employees' managers did not stress the importance of making the change or did not show a personal commitment to making the change themselves (when managers were not involved in the change or were showing resistance or uncertainty). Participants also stated that a lack of visible support from senior management contributed to employee resistance, especially when business leaders failed to communicate directly with employees or when employees lacked trust in their leaders.

5. **Job loss**
   Employees were especially fearful of any changes that could possibly affect their employment during difficult economic times.

Other notable responses:

- Some employees were resistant to change because they were not given the opportunity to actively participate in the change. Lack of involvement and engagement early in the design resulted in employees resisting change simply because they were not part of the process.

- Study participants also cited change saturation (too much change already underway) as another factor for employee resistance.

## Steps for dealing with employee resistance

Study participants suggested two main focus areas for managing employee resistance:

- Awareness of why the change is needed

- How the change would directly impact employees

**Building awareness of the business need for the change**, and the intended results, was an important step to reducing resistance. Specifically, participants recommended communicating to employees about:

- The goals of the change

- Why the change was being made

- Personal and organizational risks if no change was made

**Sharing how the change would impact and benefit employees**, including how they fit into the change, was the second area for reducing resistance. Explaining "what's in it for me" and engaging employees in conversations about the personal impact of the change were viewed as significant steps toward reducing resistance to the change. Where applicable, this included sharing the associated personal benefits or rewards.

To accomplish these objectives, study participants made recommendations in three areas:

1. **Communications**
   Open and honest two-way communications targeted toward specific groups was reported as the most effective communication method. Face-to-face sessions allowed for employee comments and interactions, and increased employee buy-in and ownership of the change. Participants noted that these communications only worked if employees felt that their concerns were being acted upon. The timing of communications was also important, as participants stated that early, timely and accurate communications worked best.

2. **Leadership involvement**
   Increased sponsor involvement, along with direct communications to employees, dramatically increased employee buy-in and support for the change. Having leadership address employee concerns swiftly and directly decreased resistance among employees. Results from the 2007 report support this tactic. In that study, participants recommended that executive sponsors provide candid, proactive and consistent messages when supporting the change and dealing with resistance. Executives and senior managers mitigated resistance by demonstrating their alignment with the change in an active and visible way while engaging subordinates in discussions about the change.

3. **The role of managers**
   Supervisors and managers were needed to provide employees with key messages about the change, to coach them through the transition and to equip them to be successful after the change was in place. Managers were critical for sharing why the change was happening and how an employee would be impacted personally. Immediate supervisors were in the best position to talk about expectations for each employee, including performance expectations that would be part of future evaluations or performance reviews. Supervisors could also discuss the consequences for not engaging in the change. This method of managing resistance was the most effective if the direct supervisor was trusted by those they were coaching. Employee resistance was also lower if their manager already supported or "bought into" the change.

Additional methods for managing employee resistance included:

- **Employee involvement and participation**
  Participants stated that resistance was less when employees were engaged in the process and when they had the opportunity to provide feedback. Direct involvement of employees increased their buy-in to the

solution, and resulted in a "positive word-of-mouth" about the change.

- **Training and mentoring programs**
  Employees felt more comfortable with a change and demonstrated less resistance when they were given the skills necessary to effectively make the change. One training method used frequently by participants was a mentoring program or the creation of networks of change agents who demonstrated the necessary skills to other employees. Another popular information sharing and training method was the use of virtual "help desks" that employees could visit to see the answers to FAQs or to see what a new process looked like before it went live.

## Avoidable employee resistance

The 2009 study included a new question aimed at understanding how much resistance was viewed as avoidable. Figure 32 shows the findings for avoidable employee resistance. Over 40% of participants indicated that more than half of employee resistance could have been avoided.

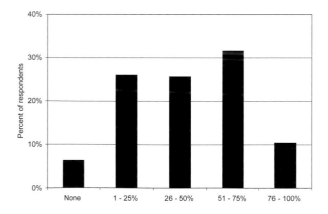

**Figure 32 – Percentage of employee resistance seen as avoidable**

## Proactive steps for avoiding or preventing resistance from employees

There were three main courses of action that study participants would have taken to proactively reduce employee resistance.

1.  **Clear, honest, two-way communications**
    Participants cited early, regular and detailed communications with all levels of employees as a way to reduce resistance. These communications should be face-to-face from supervisors and managers with consistent and structured messages, and should begin at the project's inception and continue until project completion. This approach provided a forum for employees to share their ideas and concerns. Employees wanted to give feedback about the project and wanted to receive regular updates on the project's progress.

    Participants stated that employees were interested in a detailed discussion of goals, risks and business needs of the change project to help them understand the nature of and reason for the change. Resistance would have been decreased if employees had a better understanding of how the change would impact them personally and what the benefits would be when they made the change (WIIFM). One important part in the discussion about benefits was to manage expectations so that front-line employees had a "realistic" view of what was going to happen.

2.  **Early involvement of end users in all phases of project development**
    Participants said they would have involved front-line employees in all steps of the process from planning to roll out. They would have involved employees earlier as a way to identify pockets of resistance and address pain points. They also would have included front-line employees in the planning phase so that the change was not presented as a "done deal" in which employees had limited input. This involvement would have given employees a sense of control and would have empowered them to become active participants in the change. With this early

involvement, participants said they would also have started training programs early in the project to allow employees to familiarize themselves with the future state. This early involvement would also have allowed for the roles at all levels in the organization to be identified and understood from the onset.

3. **Manager and supervisor engagement**
Participants stated that the early participation of managers and supervisors would have helped to reduce employee resistance and the likelihood that the managers and supervisors themselves would be resistant. Participants also stated that coaching managers to be change role models, or "agents of change," would have made them more accountable in the success of the change project. To establish this role, managers needed training in both the details of the change and in change management. Lastly, giving managers and supervisors the necessary authority to motivate the front-line employees through incentive programs and performance reviews would help mitigate resistance.

## Primary reasons managers resisted change

Participants in the 2009 study cited four top reasons why managers resisted change:

1. **Lack of awareness about and involvement in the change**
By far, the largest contributor to resistance from managers was a lack of understanding of the scope, timeline and impact of the change on them and on their employees. Study participants stated that managers felt left out of the project planning phase, and that their expertise and proximity to the end users was not utilized. This lack of awareness and involvement in the specifics of the project caused a lack of clarity in their roles and responsibilities in the change, and they were unsure of what was expected of them. The impression from managers was that a lack of information about the change suggested a negative impact on them and their

employees. Managers were also resistant when the benefits of the project were not clearly defined for them, especially when these benefits were only identified at the corporate level.

2. **Loss of control or negative impact on job role**
Many managers felt that the change reduced the dependence on their personal knowledge and contribution, thereby making them redundant (less needed). They felt this redundancy would cause them to lose their positions of power or lose their jobs completely. If the change was not going to result in management job loss, then managers felt that the change would cause them to fail or look incompetent because it took them out of their comfort zones or changed the way they did their job. They were also often afraid that the changes would have a negative impact on their job titles, wages and performance reviews for themselves and that of their staff.

3. **Increased workload and lack of time**
A lack of time to manage the change successfully was also a source of resistance from managers. Study participants reported that managers felt that the change itself was too cumbersome and time consuming or that they had competing priorities and had reached a point of change saturation for themselves and their employees. Managers also believed that the change would result in a decrease in productivity and an increase in workload that they would be held accountable for. At the very least, many managers saw the addition of the change as an "annoying interruption" to their day-to-day tasks.

4. **Culture of change resistance and past failures**
Another source of resistance from managers dealt with the particular culture of their organizations and the history of past change projects. Managers distrusted a particular change due to a feeling that it was "the flavor of the month" and that it would fail like past changes had failed. Another aspect of this distrust was a sense that maintaining the status quo was the safest way to prevent any of the adverse effects of a failed change. This

inertia was often due to a lack of management accountability in past initiatives.

## *Steps for dealing with manager resistance*

Study participants suggested four main ways of mitigating resistance from managers:

1. **Open a two-way dialogue about the "what and why" of the change**
   Participants cited an open two-way dialogue as the most effective way to manage resistance from managers. These targeted communications with managers were most effective when they were detailed, timely, candid and face-to-face. Participants stated that managers were interested in:

   - Reasons for the change and risks of not making the change

   - The personal and professional benefits of the change

   - A clear understanding of the goals of the project

   - A picture of the "future state"

   - Status of the project's progress

   - Information about his or her individual roles and responsibilities during the change

   Resistance was also reduced when the managers were given the opportunity to provide feedback about the change.

2. **Give managers the necessary tools and time to succeed at the change**
   Managers' resistance was reduced when they understood the change and had the necessary skills and tools to succeed at that change. Skill building included role plays and demonstrating the new processes or tools as a way to build confidence with managers. Another important factor in mitigating resistance was the timing of the change and understanding the managers' competing priorities with regard to that change. Breaking the change down into small

actionable steps and giving the managers enough time to prepare their teams helped decrease resistance. Many participants also said that the inclusion of change management training was helpful in mitigating resistance.

3. **Engage senior leadership**
   Managers were less resistant when there was active support from leadership and when they were granted the resources necessary to make the change effectively. This high level sponsorship came in the form of communications and workshops between management and the sponsors, as well as discussions about the business case for the change. Managers were more responsive in meetings with the sponsor because they felt that *"they could talk to someone who was in the position to take action on the manager's concerns."*

4. **Involve managers in all stages of the project**
   Engaging managers in all stages of the process gave them "ownership" of the change and reduced the likelihood and strength of resistance. Early involvement allowed the managers to become "agents" of the change and made them "part of the solution, not the problem." Managers were also less likely to be resistant when their "subject matter expertise" was tapped in the development of the change project. It made them feel like the change was happening with them, not to them.

## Avoidable manager resistance

Figure 33 shows the findings for avoidable resistance by managers. Over 40% of participants felt that more than half of the resistance from managers was avoidable.

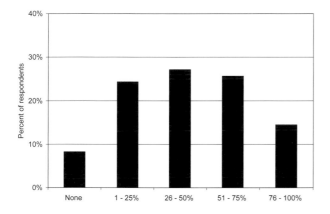

**Figure 33 – Percentage of manager resistance seen as avoidable**

## Proactive steps for avoiding or preventing resistance from managers and supervisors

Participants provided three main action steps for proactively addressing manager and supervisor resistance:

1. **Management involvement in all phases of the project**
   Participants cited the early engagement of managers in the development and planning stages of the project as the number one proactive step they could have taken to prevent management resistance. This involvement included:

   - Asking for and using their feedback in the project plan

   - Creating an understanding of their role in the change from the onset

   - Making them part of the "communication cascade" to inform their employees of the change

This early involvement would have made the managers "change agents" and also would have made them responsible for the success of the change.

2. **Early awareness building**
   Another factor that participants cited as a proactive step for avoiding managers' resistance was building managers' awareness of the benefits of the change and the overall strategy. They recommended detailed and frequent communications even when all the details were not known to keep the managers "in the loop." These communications would make the case for the change and explain the impact of the change on managers and their employees.

3. **Executive support**
   Participants cited active executive support as another important factor in preventing management resistance. This support came in several forms:

   - Detailed explanation of the strategy and business case for making the change

   - Consistent focus on the project and making the project's priority clear to managers

   - Understanding of, and help dealing with, competing workload issues

## Identifying resistance from employees and managers

Participants were asked to identify what resistance to change looked like. The top responses were:

1. **Lack of participation**
   Lack of participation was most commonly seen in employees trying to outlast the change – waiting for it to "go away" like previously attempted changes. Study participants also observed groups of employees trying to be excused or exempted from adopting the new processes.

   *"Same old, same old – this will go away like everything else has, just another 'flavor of the month'."*

2. **Openly expressing emotion**
Negative emotional expression took many forms including complaining, criticism, nitpicking, hostility, aggression, anger, frustration, excuses, low morale, bad attitudes, critical comments and openly expressing doubts that the change would work.

3. **Lack of attendance and absenteeism**
Lack of attendance was seen in three different ways: not attending status meetings and project events, not attending scheduled trainings and being absent from work altogether.

4. **Reverting to old ways**
Employees would ignore the new ways of doing work and find work-arounds.

5. **A decrease in productivity and missed deadlines**
A noticeable reduction in work output or delays could be observed.

Participants also identified what resistance to change looked like when exhibited by executives and top managers, including:

1. **Unwillingness to sponsor the change**
Executives who were resistant to the change did not openly endorse the project, did not attend key events or meetings, showed skepticism with subordinates and did not build a coalition of support.

    *"Senior leadership agreed with the change at a very high level, but did very little to cascade and to get business buy-in."*

2. **Reluctance to provide resources and information**
Executives and top managers showed resistance to projects by not assigning staff to support the change or by withholding information needed for project progress and success.

    *"Sharing limited information and discouraging staff from taking on additional responsibilities."*

Source date: 2007

## Who was most resistant to change?

Participants in the 2007 study identified mid-level managers as the most resistant group to change (Figure 34), a finding that echoed the results in the 2005 benchmarking study.

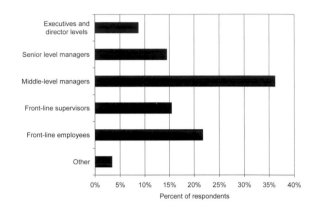

**Figure 34 – Most resistant groups**

Source date: 2007

## Ineffective methods for dealing with resistance

Participants cited the top five mistakes to avoid when managing resistance.

1. **Ignoring resistance and expecting it to go away on its own**
Participants overwhelming cited ignoring resistance as the biggest mistake. Ignoring or avoiding resistance did not make it go away and in some cases made it worse.

2. **Not listening to and understanding the concerns of those impacted**
Participants said that not understanding the root cause of resistance prevented them from responding to the real issues and led to the conclusion that all resistance is the same. This led to an ineffective "one-size-fits-all" approach to managing resistance. Next time, participants said they would not assume all behavior was a result of resistance, but instead would work to listen to impacted employees and ask questions to understand

the root causes and reasons for their behavior.

*"Not fully understanding the nature of the resistance and the factors leading to it, and trying to apply a 'one approach fits all' mindset."*

3. **Not gaining input from those impacted**
Participants stated that applying force and pressure from the top down to implement a change was a mistake for managing resistance. This approach did not build the buy-in and engagement of those impacted and therefore made it difficult to manage resistance.

*"Shutting resistors out – they may have some valuable contributions despite the resistance."*

4. **Underestimating the resistance**
Underestimating the resistance to change was cited as a significant mistake by participants because it resulted in a lack of planning for the change. This lack of planning was felt most significantly in the areas of building executive sponsorship and securing their involvement.

5. **Poor communications**
Poor communications made managing resistance very difficult. Poor communications included inconsistent messages, incorrect messages, incorrect senders, bad timing and dishonest information. Participants also stated that using a public forum to confront a resistor was a mistake.

Source date: 2007

## *Impacts of using pain or fear to manage change*

Study participants overwhelmingly agreed that using fear or pain to manage change was not sustainable in the long term. Some participants acknowledged that using fear or pain may catalyze change or create "movement," but that this effect was short-lasted. They stated that if fear was used as part of the awareness message to employees, the threat to the organization must be real and visible.

Participants also stated that if fear or pain was used repeatedly as a tool to drive change, employees began to lose trust in the message (the "boy who cried wolf" scenario) and lose confidence in the organization's leadership. Study participants listed a number of likely consequences from managing change with fear or pain including:

- Increased employee turnover (including losing the best employees)
- Lower productivity
- Higher resistance
- Slower adoption of the change

For the most part, study participants agreed that fear or pain as a resistance management tool alienated employees and created resentment. Employee morale was impacted and people became cynical towards the organization, leadership and the change.

Editor's note. A distinction should be made by the reader between using fear or pain on a personal level to motivate a person to change, and the natural worry or fear that can result from building awareness about the seriousness of a situation that is present in an organization. The distinction being made here is whether fear is being used as an intentional tool or weapon to manage resistance, as compared to a natural response to a real and observable condition.

Source date: 2007

# Reinforcement and feedback

## Who should provide reinforcement?

The employee's direct supervisor was cited by nearly 40% of 2007 study participants as the best provider of reinforcement, followed by the primary sponsor (Figure 35).

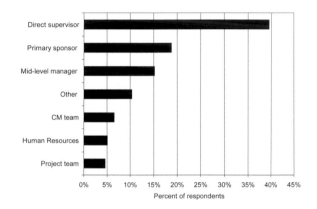

**Figure 35 – Preferred providers of reinforcement**

Source date: 2007

## Most effective ways to reinforce change at the group level

Participants cited the following approaches as the most effective ways to reinforce groups dealing with change:

1. **Celebrations of project successes**
   Participants indicated that it was important to celebrate successes when groups pass project milestones or achieve a certain level of performance. Celebrations could be large public events or smaller, team-focused or department-focused gatherings.

2. **Formal recognition of group contributions**
   Acknowledge the contributions made by groups with formal recognition from managers and executives at meetings and company events or in organization-wide newsletters or emails.

*"In general, people like to see their name in communication, especially linked to success."*

3. **Performance measurement**
   Track key metrics related to the change projects and keep employees updated on their performance during the transition and after implementation. Participants suggested using a dashboard or scorecard approach to measure employee compliance and performance.

4. **Frequent communications**
   Maintain frequent communications with employees during the change. Messages should focus on the status of the change project and continue to reinforce the business reasons for making the change, the benefits already realized, success stories and consequences of not changing.

5. **Feedback opportunities**
   Give employees multiple opportunities to offer input, concerns and other feedback throughout the life of the project. Regular feedback meetings, town hall sessions, email and message boards were cited as examples of effective feedback approaches by participants.

Source date: 2007

## Most effective ways to reinforce change at an individual level

Participants cited the following responses as the most effective ways for managers and supervisors to reinforce change with individual employees:

1. **Recognition of efforts**
   Recognize employees for their individual contributions. Participants suggested using both public and private recognition. Examples of public recognition include acknowledgment at a staff meeting or credit given in organization-wide emails or newsletters. Private recognition could simply

be a personal "thank you" from a manager or senior leader.

*"Telling someone enthusiastically that they did a good job goes a long way."*

2. **One-on-one discussions**
Use personal conversations and encourage a dialogue with employees about the change. Be open and honest in these discussions.

3. **Rewards**
Provide deserving employees with tangible rewards, such as bonuses, promotions or gifts. Rewards could also include small, inexpensive gestures, such as free lunches or additional vacation days.

4. **Performance measurement system**
Align change compliance to individual performance goals. This technique holds employees accountable for working in the "new way" and rewards them for achieving success.

5. **Feedback opportunities**
Offer multiple opportunities and channels for individuals to provide feedback throughout the change project. Examples cited by participants included executive walk-arounds, email addresses and bulletin boards specifically designated for project feedback.

Source date: 2007

## Most effective methods for determining if employees were engaged

Participants identified three methods to determine employee engagement in a change:

1. **Face-to-face communications**
Responses heavily favored face-to-face meetings and discussions as the clearest indicator of employee engagement. Interviews with employees, including questions related to their understanding of the change and its impact on their roles and the organization, were key in gauging involvement. A number of participants incorporated written surveys into their process to evaluate employee attitudes related to the change.

2. **Metrics and performance feedback**
Participants relied on data to validate engagement by employees. Metrics and supervisor feedback were instrumental in identifying the speed of adoption and engagement of the work force. Some organizations tested employees for procedural knowledge and process implementation. Several participants said Key Performance Indicators (KPIs) were in place to monitor acceptance of new processes.

*"The numbers speak the loudest."*

3. **Observation**
Observing employees in their working environment was another good indicator of engagement. Questions to consider when observing employee behavior included:

- Are they modeling the desired behavior?
- Are they solving unexpected problems?
- Are they displaying a willing attitude?

Source date: 2007

## Mistakes to avoid when reinforcing change

Participants offered their recommendations of what to avoid when reinforcing change with employees. The majority of the input pertained to three primary areas:

- Rewards and recognition
- Two-way communications
- The link between change and performance

### Avoid awards or recognition that are not meaningful to employees

Rewarding employees to reinforce desired behaviors and attitudes is an important element to sustaining change. However, one size does not fit all. Advice from participants was to:

- Make it meaningful and genuine – if it is contrived, it won't survive

*"Don't broad-brush 'thanks' or 'good job', be specific about each person's contribution."*

- Include everyone – overlooking individuals creates disengagement

  *"Avoid the hero syndrome."*

- Make it timely – celebrate small wins along the way rather than waiting until the end

  *"Find the balance. Too much is just as bad as too little."*

### Avoid impersonal, one-way communications

Participants indicated they would have worked harder to create two-way discussions with individuals that allowed a better feedback loop. The recommendation from participants was to isolate confrontational issues and resistors for one-on-one discussions. Public displays with ultimatums were disengaging.

### Don't assume that the change will just happen

Participants felt the need to hold employees accountable to the change and not allow them to slip back to the old way of doing work. Developing goals at the individual level was an effective way to make the change part of everyday business. They also recommended establishing metrics, considering role changes and rewriting performance measures to link new processes to pay.

*"Presume nothing – check everything."*

*"What gets measured gets done. So establish a measurement system and advertise the results regularly."*

Other notable suggestions included:

- Address problems promptly

- Allow employees time to adjust – do not forget the time needed for learning

Source date: 2007

## How can performance appraisals and measures encourage change adoption?

Participants indicated that performance appraisals, which link the business goals to individual performance, can enhance change adoption by:

- **Clarifying roles and expectations for every employee**
  Goals that are specific and focused on individual contributions remove uncertainty and provide the necessary structure for employees to support new business objectives.

  *"Structure drives behavior, so make sure how people are measured and rewarded supports the strategy and expected behaviors of the company."*

- **Rewarding change adopters in an equitable manner**
  Employees quickly recognize the value placed on change when it is tied to pay. Incentives that go hand-in-hand with performance increase the likelihood of enhanced outcomes.

- **Creating an accountability model**
  Goals tied to performance and business objectives allow managers to check, correct and celebrate wins along the way.

- **Identifying and managing resistance**
  Performance appraisals can effectively address and offer consequences for non-compliance.

In addition to using performance appraisals to reinforce change, more than one half of participants cited using new job descriptions as an additional mechanism to reinforce change.

Source date: 2007

# Consultants

## *Use of consultants*

Nearly one half of participants in the 2009 study used an external consultant to support their change management work.

## *Primary role played by consultants*

The top five roles played by consultants supporting change management activities were:

1. **Provide training and impart knowledge**
   More than any other role, consultants were hired to provide change management training and impart their own change management expertise. They were asked to educate employees, management and executives on topics such as change management methodology, change strategy, resistance management and changing an organization's "state of mind."

2. **Change management lead**
   The second most common role consultants were asked to fill was that of change management lead. They were asked to create the change management plan(s) and take responsibility for any and all change management activities.

3. **Mentor/coach/HR support**
   A number of consultants were asked to fill the role of a mentor or coach. Responses implied a closer connection with the people involved with the change. During planning and execution, the consultants were expected to provide support and feedback, often at what seemed to be a more emotional level, such as being a "cheerleader" or "keeping fire under their toes." Other aspects of these consultants' roles were sponsor alignment and coaching and addressing human resources type issues, like mediation and conflict resolution.

4. **Advisor**
   A number of consultants acted as advisors during change initiatives. Study participants relied on these consultants to apply readiness and present-state assessments as well as long term assessments and recommendations during the course of an initiative. A few scheduled only weekly visits with an organization. Although less connected to the people involved in the change initiative, these consultants were aware of what was going on and knowledgeable in change management and its processes.

5. **Assist in or create communications regarding the change and change management**
   Consultants were relied on for creating and disseminating communications regarding a change initiative. It was noted that they assisted with the communication between executives, managers and employees alike.

## *Criteria for choosing a change management consultant*

Participants were asked to identify the primary criteria used for selecting the change management consultant they hired. The top four responses were:

- **Consulting company's qualifications**
  These included both tangible and intangible qualities. Participants looked at the company's longevity, experience and references. However, intangible qualities also came into play. These included a consulting firm's ability to work as part of a team in the existing company culture, their interpersonal skills, work ethic and being judged a "good fit" for the organization.

- **Project management skills and knowledge, or experience in subject area**
  Some organizations placed priority on a consulting firm's experience with similar projects or technical expertise in the area of the change. Often, consultants were already involved in the technical side of the change or the project management aspect of the change, so they were asked to follow through with the people side of the change.

- **Change management expertise and use of a certain methodology**
  Many organizations gave weight to a consulting company's expertise in change management and its use of a proven change management methodology. One participant commented, *"I was told by my client that she didn't know what she wanted or needed but when I began to talk about change management processes and ideas in the interview, she knew that was it!"*

- **Existing relationship**
  Some change leaders did not have to select a consulting company. Their organizations already had an established relationship, or even a contract, with a consultant. If they were happy with the consultant's past performance, they were content to retain that firm for change management support.

## Why did you use a consultant?

By a five-to-one margin, participants cited a lack of internal expertise in change management as the primary motivator for hiring a consultant. The top factors were:

- Lack of internal expertise

- Lack of resources from inside the organization

- Need for an external perspective

In some cases, a consultant was used because the project leader had previous experience with the consultant or an executive had already decided to use a consultant to support the change.

Source date: 2007

## Why did you choose not to hire a consultant?

Participants who did not use a consultant shared their reasoning for not bringing in external support. Overwhelmingly, they cited an existing internal change management competency as the primary reason. The top reasons for not using a consultant as cited by participants were:

1. **Internal competency and skills existed**
   Many participants cited having sufficient internal knowledge and skills for managing change. Some utilized internal change management experts while others trained their staff in change management for the project.

2. **Not in the budget**
   The second most common response was the high cost for external change management support that was not allocated for in the budget.

3. **No perceived need**
   The project team did not perceive additional value in bringing in external support for the change management effort.

4. **Greater employee buy-in**
   Some participants felt that they could create greater commitment from employees by handling change management activities internally. There was a perceived value to using internal resources. There were also potential hurdles related to getting an external consultant familiar with the cultural setting and project.

*"The change should not come from consultants but from the employees and managers."*

Source date: 2007

## Consultants used

Participants in the 2009 study provided a list of consultants they used for their projects. Those mentioned by more than one participant are indicated with an asterisk (*).

- 3rd i Consulting
- Accenture*
- Accelare
- Accretive Solutions
- A.C.T. Advanced Consulting and Technology
- Adams-Gabbert and Associates, LLC
- Adaptive Management Consultants
- African Synergies
- Alex Apouchtine
- Al-Musaned
- Archstone
- ARGOS Consulting Firm
- Artis Rei
- Astral Consulting
- AT Kearney
- Atos-Origin*
- Axis People Management
- Bartholomew Corporate Solutions
- Bearing Point*
- Being Human*
- BES consultants
- BlessingWhite
- Blue Heron Consulting
- Booz Allen Hamilton*
- BRIDGES, Inc.
- Cal y Mayor y Asociados
- California Manufacturing Technology Consulting
- CapGemini*
- Carbon Group
- Cegedim
- Centna Consulting Limited
- Cepeda Systems & Software Analysis, Inc
- CGI*
- Chameleon Adventure Academy
- Change Consultoria
- Change Guides
- Change Worx
- Changewright Consulting
- Ciber*
- Clarkston Consulting
- CMTC
- Collective Next
- COMED IT
- Competitive Capabilities International
- Conner Partners
- Cue 7 Consortium
- Courtyard Group
- Croken Enterprises
- Crystalmount Solutions, Inc
- CSC*
- David White
- Dawit Giorgis/African Crisis team
- DDI
- De Adviespraktijk
- Delegata
- Deloitte*
- Destin
- Dreamhouse Consulting, LLC
- DSD Laboratories, Inc
- EduServe
- Emerson Human Capital*
- Enaxis Consulting LP
- Enmasse services
- Enterprise Transformation Group Ltd.
- EQE Bulgaria AD
- Ernest and Young*
- Ethiopian Management Institute
- Firestone International Associates, Inc
- FMA Process Engineering
- Focusphera Consulting
- Frank McGrath Change Management Ltd
- Fujitsu
- GAR Organizational Solutions
- GSS Holdings
- Harriss Wagner Management Consultants
- HCL Axon
- Highveld PFS
- Hitachi Consulting*
- HO team
- HP
- Humadyn
- iB4e
- IBM*
- Incahoots Consultancy
- Infosys*
- Ink Business Development Services Ltd.
- Innovapost
- Insightrix
- Integral Insights
- Interlinks consult
- Jalellpea Television
- John Dorris
- John Mant
- Keane Inc
- Kenya Water Institute
- KMAC

- KPMG
- La Societe conseil Lambda Inc
- LaMarsh and Associates*
- Langford and Oliver Consulting
- LeftField Project Solutions
- Leonardo Schvarstein
- Lighthouse Institute
- Linium
- LM Dulye and Co
- Logica
- Management Effect
- MAP Consulting
- MARSH Risk Consulting
- McDougall Smith
- McKinsey and Company
- Mdb Consulting
- Modal
- North Highland*
- Nelson Consulting Group
- Oakton*
- Online Business Systems
- Oracle
- P2
- Paradigma
- PCGI Consulting Inc.
- Pearce Delport
- People and Process Management
- People Firm
- People First
- PeopleNRG
- Performance Path
- Performance republic international
- Perot Systems
- POLITEC
- PriceWaterHouseCoopers*
- Proacteur*
- ProFitness Advisors
- Progressor Consulting
- Project SI
- PSTG
- Pulse Development Services
- Qedis Consulting
- QMS
- Quatum West
- RAMSE Consulting
- Resources Global Professionals
- Revere Froup
- RWD Technologies*
- S1 Consulting
- SAIC
- Saje Consulting
- Salalah College of Technology
- Satreno Change Management
- Satyam*
- See Results, Inc.
- SHL Group

- SHMA
- Sirius Solutions LLP
- Solution Dynamics
- Son Systems
- Stegmeier Consulting Group
- Successworks
- Superior Directions
- TASC Management Consulting, LLC
- Tata Consulting Services
- TCS
- The Carey Group
- The Centre for Personnel Transformation
- The Change Experience
- The Hackett Group
- The Urwick Group
- TMA
- UCS Solutions
- Ultima Consulting Firm
- University of Tennessee Center for Industrial Services
- Vicky Coates and Associates
- WDScott
- Wilson Learning*
- Wipro

# Project management and change management integration

A new section was added to the 2009 study to better understand the integration of change management and project management.

## *Perception of change management by project teams*

Overall, 58% of participants reported that their project teams felt that change management was either critical or necessary (Figure 36). However, there were still over 40% of participants who indicated that their project team either viewed change management as just another activity to do (31%) or as a nuisance with no value (11%).

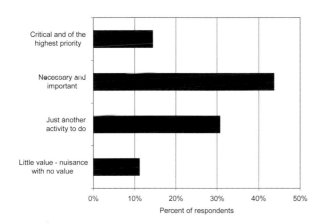

**Figure 36 – Project teams' view of the role of change management**

## *Steps to engage project team in change management*

Participants identified a number of effective steps taken to engage the project team in change management. The top eight tactics in rank order were:

1. **Working collaboratively with the project team**
   Participants cited numerous ways that the project team and change management team could work in collaboration. Responses

included actions for the project team and actions for the change management team.

- Actions for the project team included getting the project team involved in change management tasks, reviews and decisions; getting the project team to sign off on change management work and participating in workshops on the people side issues of the project.

- Actions for the change management team included taking part in project meetings; providing one-on-one coaching and mentoring to project team members; being involved in the development and planning work on the project; providing information to the project team from change management assessments and stakeholder evaluations and participating in decision making.

- A number of participants also cited the importance of team building and relationships so that the two groups worked as a single, cross-functional team sharing accountability and responsibility for project outcomes.

2. **Making a compelling case for why change management is necessary**
   An important approach for engaging the project team was to make a compelling case for why change management is needed. This included highlighting that change management is necessary for achieving results and is a valuable undertaking. Some participants focused on how change management would make the project team's job easier and remove some of the barriers and pain points they faced. Others focused on the role that behavioral and process changes would play in the project and the potential consequences, like increased resistance, that could happen if the people side of change was managed poorly. Looking at past changes and highlighting the role that change management played in successes, or pointing out the failures that resulted from ignoring

change management, was another approach mentioned by participants.

3. **Providing training and education**
Provide the project team with change management education and make them aware of the process that would be followed and the role and impact of change management.

4. **Making change management "real" to project teams**
A number of participants said that change management had to be tied to the work the project team did to be successful. This included talking about change management using the language and terminology of the project team, directly linking it to project work, focusing on deliverables and clarifying the outcomes and activities of change management.

5. **Integrating change management activities into the project plan**
Project teams were more engaged when the change management activities could be integrated into the already existing project activities.

6. **Leveraging sponsor involvement**
Senior leaders could encourage project team engagement by demonstrating their support for utilizing change management. In some cases, senior leaders insisted on change management for the project.

7. **Communicating**
The change management team used deliberate communication efforts with the project team on key change management topics and issues.

8. **Documenting of roles and responsibilities**
Clearly documenting the role of both the change management team and the project team helped facilitate engagement.

## *Project management integration on projects*

While only 60% of participants stated that they used a structured methodology for managing the people side of change, 86% reported applying a structured project management approach to the change (Figure 37).

**Figure 37 – Did the project you reported on for this study apply project management?**

Over 80% of the participants integrated change management activities into the project activities (Figure 38).

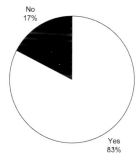

**Figure 38 – Did you integrate change management activities into the project activities?**

## Obstacles with project team

Participants were asked to identify the biggest obstacles they faced when introducing change management to the project team. The top five obstacles cited were:

1. **Did not see the importance of change management**
   The project team did not view change management as an important part of project success. They were not convinced change management was necessary and did not see the risk of ignoring the people side of change. They considered it the "soft" or "fuzzy" work and saw no real benefit. Change management was perceived as a waste of time or as a luxury.

2. **Lack of knowledge and understanding of change management**
   The project team did not understand what change management really was. In some cases, they equated change management with training or communications. Change management was viewed as simply an activity to "check off" upon completion.

3. **No budget, resources or time to do change management**
   Change management was seen as too costly and often no budget existed for change management activities. Resource constraints on the project team meant no one was available to focus on change management and the team found it difficult to make the time for change management activities.

4. **Role confusion**
   Role confusion existed around change management. In some cases, the team did not understand their role or the role change management would play in the project. In other cases, change management was seen as someone else's responsibility and not the responsibility of the project team.

5. **Assumption that change management slowed down the project**
   A number of participants indicated that the project team felt that using change management would hamper the progress of the project. Typically these concerns revolved around impeding progress, slowing down the project or causing changes in the timeline of the project. Several participants also noted that the project team saw change management as additional and burdensome work.

Other responses on obstacles with the project team included:

- Confusion on how to integrate change management and project activities

- Change management was a new and difficult concept to grasp

- The project team did not see or appreciate the people side of the change they were managing

- Change management was not a priority

## What would you do differently on the next project regarding integrating change management into project activities?

Participants provided a number of suggestions regarding what they would do differently in terms of change management and project activity integration. The top five suggestions were:

1. **Begin change management earlier**
   By a two-to-one margin, participants suggested starting change management at the onset of the project. By starting change management earlier, at the initiation of the project, change management and project activities were more easily integrated.

   *"Have a CM person in the initiating phase of the program to have enough time to design a proper program instead of having to retro-fit and catch up."*

2. **Provide training on change management**
   More change management training and educational workshops for project team members allowed for better partnership and integration. When project team members understood change management, they were

3. **Ensure adequate resources for change management**
   There were several suggestions regarding resources. The first was the designation of a change management resource for the project, including the option of hiring a change manager. Participants also commented on the importance of having qualified, experienced practitioners doing the change management work. In addition to the human resource component, participants mentioned ensuring that time and budget was available for change management work.

4. **Engage senior leaders**
   Senior leaders were important on two fronts. The first was engaging senior leaders in the importance and necessity of change management so they could support it during the project. The second aspect was ensuring adequate sponsorship and leadership involvement during the project itself. A number of participants indicated that they would have the change management resource report directly to senior leaders.

5. **Engage with project members**
   Engaging the project team involved both building the case for change management and working in conjunction on the project. Participants indicated that they had to "sell" the story of change management to their project managers to ensure they understood the need for effectively managing the people side of change. Participants also provided tactical suggestions including having the project team work in partnership on change management issues, sitting in with the project team, being more involved in the technical side of the change and ensuring that the project leader takes accountability and ownership of change management issues like user adoption and acceptance.

Additional suggestions included:

- Fully integrate plans into a holistic, single project plan that included all change management and project management deliverables

- Clarify responsibilities for the change management group and the project team members regarding change management

- Utilize a formal change management approach and methodology

## Change management training for project team

Participants shared the percentage of the project team that had training in change management (Figure 39). Nearly two thirds of the study participants indicated that 25% or less of the project team had been trained in change management. About 10% of study participants said the entire project team had training in change management.

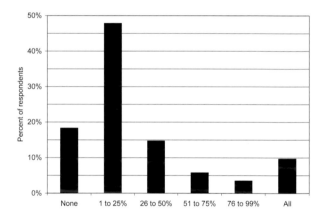

**Figure 39 – Percentage of project team with change management training**

# Change readiness

## Identifying change readiness

Study participants used three primary methods to assess their organization's readiness for change:

1. **Written assessments/surveys** were favored by half of all responding. They used a variety of tools to gather information, including a readiness assessment, business impact assessment, change characteristics and organizational attributes assessment, SWOT analysis, gap analysis, perception survey, stakeholder analysis and a change portfolio assessment.

2. **Interviews** with senior leaders, key stakeholders, managers and staff were mentioned by one fourth of the study participants. Some study participants referred to these as "alignment interviews." They also mentioned the benefit of having one-on-one interactions and being able to have discussions informally and confidentially to gain insight.

3. **Focus groups and meetings** were also cited as a means to identify the readiness of an organization to make a change.

*"We have a very formal process for assessing results. We have focus groups, but then we run large full day workshops to review readiness starting 12 weeks out from go-live involving all project team members and operational representatives. Readiness of each functional area is rated on a traffic light system and risks and issues are identified and highlighted. The output from these sessions is reported up to the management team. This process is repeated at 8 weeks, 4 weeks, and 2 weeks [prior to the go-live date]."*

## Readiness assessment factors

When formally assessing organizational readiness for change, study participants were asked for the most important areas to consider. The top factors in rank order were:

1. **Assessing whether a clear and concise business need for change is understood at all levels of the organization**
   Do the employees know the risks of not changing, understand the challenges ahead and have the desire to move forward?

2. **Assessing the change legacy of the organization**
   Does past history indicate a culture of successful or failed change? Is the culture open to change or averse to change?

   *"Change-agile as a core value."*

3. **Assessing the style and ability of the sponsor to champion the change**
   Is the sponsor influential, engaging and trusted within the organization? Is the sponsor aware of the important role he/she will play in leading the change effort?

   *"Leadership ability to shepherd the change."*

4. **Assessing the amount of change occurring in the organization**
   Is the climate in constant flux, fatigued, saturated or enduring competing initiatives?

Additional factors mentioned included:
- Funding and resources
- Communication effectiveness
- Management involvement
- Change management knowledge
- Resistance
- Clearly defined future state
- Complexity of the change
- Training requirements of the workforce
- Processes to support the change
- Time
- Ability to change
- ROI

## Readiness evaluation

Over 60% of participants took steps to evaluate the readiness of the organization for their particular change (Figure 40).

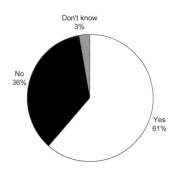

**Figure 40 – Took steps to evaluate change readiness**

## Main organizational barriers or challenges

Study participants reported a variety of organizational barriers and challenges when implementing change. The top five barriers in rank order were:

1. **Lack of buy-in**
   Employees from all levels of the organization did not understand the business need for change and, as a result, were disinterested in the change, reluctant to take ownership and resistant to participating in the change. They wanted to know "What's in it for me?"

2. **Organizational culture**
   A culture of complacency, conservatism and laissez-faire attitudes created challenges. Many reported their organizations as being slow-movers accustomed to the same old way where change was counter-cultural.

   *"100 year history of growth and success without change."*

3. **The structure of the organization**
   Large organizations struggled with the sheer number of people involved; some organizations were bureaucratic and complex and others faced geographic/global spread which created unique challenges.

4. **Lack of change management knowledge and expertise**
   Participants cited a need for a consistent approach, an internal change management competency and an overall change management strategy.

   *"We don't know how to start. We don't have any experience on how to manage the change."*

5. **Lack of an effective leader and sponsor of change**
   Study participants said they needed a decisive leader who was enthusiastic about the change. They needed a real sponsor willing to lead and visibly support the change.

Study participants shared other organizational barriers including:

- A history of failed change

- Limited resources and funding

- Change fatigue and saturation

- Competing priorities

- "Siloed" departments/organizations

# Justifying change management

Over half of the study participants indicated that they had to justify change management to their leadership team (Figure 41).

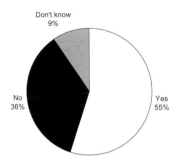

Don't know
9%

No
36%

Yes
55%

**Figure 41 – Percentage of participants who had to justify change management to leadership team**

Participants who needed to justify change management to their senior leaders used one or more of the following tactics:

1. **Learned from past failures**
   Study participants discussed recent project failures, especially those that people would remember and acknowledge did not go well, to demonstrate the risks and financial impacts of poorly managed change (used real-life practical examples).

2. **Clearly showed the negative consequences of poorly managed change**
   Participants quantified the impact of "what can go wrong" and identified the potential risks to the organization if change management was not implemented effectively.

   *"We created 'what if' scenarios to demonstrate the potential consequences of poorly managed change."*

3. **Translated change management into tangible financial impacts**
   Participants linked change management to

the ability to maximize project outcomes and focused all discussions on business results.

4. **Presented the outcomes of successful projects that used change management**
   Study participants contrasted successful projects with projects that did not use change management and were less successful.

5. **Used data to connect change management to the return on investment (ROI)**
   Participants provided senior managers with external research data that showed the correlation of financial success of a change project (or meeting project objectives) with the effectiveness of change management.

Some additional tactics participants shared were:

- Quantified potential impacts of employee turnover and productivity loss from poorly managed change

- Presented case studies and data from other companies that had used change management (benchmarking data was used to build credibility)

- Gained direct support of one senior leader who then became an advocate and spokesperson for change management with other business leaders

   *"Found a few change champions."*

- Connected change management activities to the specific outcomes that their business leaders were trying to achieve

- Gathered feedback from employees using surveys or interviews to show the negative impacts of poorly managed change; used organizational readiness assessments to demonstrate the impact of change management

- Used a current, real project as a testing ground or trial to show the effectiveness of change management

- Brought in a credible, outside speaker to provide an executive briefing to senior leaders on change management and why it is important for business success

- Integrated change management with project management and focused the discussion on the overall business objectives (not simply on the value of change management alone)

Participants who did *not* have to justify change management as part of their change project cited the presence of one or more the following conditions:

- Past results with change management were very positive, preventing any further need to justify change management activities.

- Sponsors already believed in the need for change management or they specifically asked for change management to be implemented as part of the project.

- The project team or project leader was very experienced with change projects and made change management part of the project activities.

- Acknowledgement that past failures resulted from a lack of effective change management, and leaders did not want to see these mistakes repeated.

- Change management was already part of the requirements and process for implementing change.

# Enterprise Change Management

## *Change Management Maturity Model*

As in the 2007 study, participants in the 2009 study indicated their organization's level on the Prosci Change Management Maturity Model. The levels of the Change Management Maturity Model rank the overall deployment and maturity of change management within an organization:

> Level 5: Organizational competency
>
> Level 4: Organizational standards
>
> Level 3: Multiple projects
>
> Level 2: Isolated projects
>
> Level 1: Absent or ad hoc

Overall, the distribution of maturity levels was fairly similar to the findings in the 2007 study (Figure 42). 85% of participants in the 2009 study indicated Level 1, Level 2 or Level 3, compared to 86% in the 2007 study. Again, Level 2 was the most cited maturity model level with almost half of all participants (47%) indicating that change management took place on isolated projects throughout the organization.

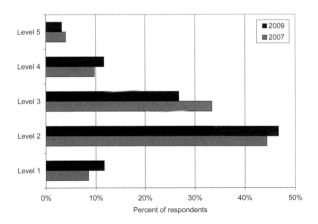

**Figure 42 – Level in the Prosci Change Management Maturity Model**

## *Percentage of projects using change management*

Participants were asked to estimate the percentage of projects in their organization that were using change management (Figure 43). More than half of the reporting organizations were applying change management on less than 25% of their change projects. Only 5% indicated that no projects were applying change management, while 4% stated that all of the projects in the organization were applying change management.

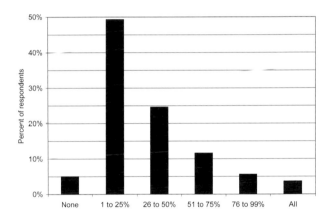

**Figure 43 – Percentage of projects within a given organization applying change management**

---

## Change management requirement on new projects

Just under one third of participants indicated that change management was a requirement for new projects (Figure 44).

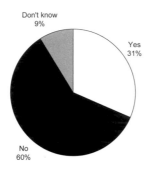

Don't know
9%

Yes
31%

No
60%

**Figure 44 – Change management requirement on new projects**

## Standard change management methodology

In the 2009 study, 43% of participants indicated they had a standard organizational methodology, up from 29% in the 2007 study (Figure 45).

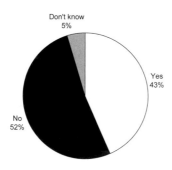

Don't know
5%

Yes
43%

No
52%

**Figure 45 – Adopted standard change management methodology**

## Top ten steps for deploying change management across an organization

Participants reported on the steps they were taking to deploy change management. Below are the most frequently cited activities for deploying change management across the organization. Responses are listed in rank order, not chronologically.

1. Train people in the organization
2. Create a change management group
3. Integrate change management into project management
4. Select a common approach for the organization
5. Assign change management resources to projects
6. Implement measurement mechanisms
7. Initiate change management at project launch
8. Mandate the use of change management
9. Enlist senior leadership support
10. Attach change management to particular projects

1. **Train people in the organization**
   Overwhelmingly, participants cited training as the top deployment approach, with special programs developed for senior leaders, project teams and supervisors. Change management was also included as a core leadership competency for the organization.

   *"Developing a change management core curriculum for every level of the enterprise."*

2. **Create a change management group**
   The change management group was a structure where change practitioners could meet and work together. There were a variety of names used including: Group of Practice, Center of Excellence, Community of Practice, Change Champions and Change Management Team. The group typically

supported both the rollout and application of change management.

3. **Integrate change management into project management**
A number of participants provided approaches for integrating change management and project management. Some interwove the methodologies, while others sequenced change management to the standard project life cycle. The Project Management Office (PMO) was sometimes seen as a resource for change management deployment.

4. **Select a common approach for the organization**
Participants identified or developed a standard approach for change management to be used on projects across the organization. This approach was communicated to project teams.

5. **Assign change management resources to projects**
A number of participants reported that they created a more consultative function for change management in the organization, including training internal change management consultants to support particular projects.

6. **Implement measurement mechanisms**
Measurement of change management efforts served to reinforce change management usage and provided results, success stories and feedback that could be shared across the organization. In addition, measurement was seen as a way to ensure compliance when applying the change management approach.

7. **Initiate change management at project launch**
Participants provided a number of suggestions for ensuring that change management was started at the launch of a project. Some made a change management plan a qualifier in the approval process (required for sign-off by project sponsors). Others took a less forward approach, working stakeholder analysis and change impact analysis into early project work and meetings.

8. **Mandate the use of change management**
A number of participants cited an executive mandate that change management must be applied and all projects must have a change management plan.

9. **Enlist senior leadership support**
Some participants used senior leaders as sponsors for implementing change management. While this was number nine on the list of approaches, it was number one on the list of what teams would do differently.

10. **Attach change management to particular projects**
Suggestions for attaching change management to particular projects included starting with large, visible, enterprise-wide changes or determining specific pilot projects for the initial application of change management.

Source date: 2007

## Most important or highest impact deployment activities

Participants identified the most important or highest impact activities for deploying change management in their organization. As with the section on steps for deployment, training was cited as the most critical deployment step. The five most effective deployment activities were:

1. **Train people in change management**
This recommendation included providing training to all levels in the organization.

2. **Enable project teams and managers to experience change management**
Actually applying the methodology helped organizations and individuals adopt and support it. Mandating change management on all projects helped increase the number of individuals exposed to change management.

3. **Demonstrate senior leader commitment**
Senior leader commitment to change management had to come from both the person leading the deployment effort and other leaders from across the different business units and functions.

4. **Show the need for change management**
Part of showing the need for change management was surfacing and acknowledging the gaps in current performance. Additionally, participants suggested clearly communicating the value of managing change effectively and how it benefited projects and the organization.

5. **Select a common methodology or approach**
Having a common approach to change management showed the organization's commitment to managing change. It also ensured greater consistency in application. Several participants cited the importance of having a methodology that was easy to use and accessible.

Other activities mentioned by participants included creating the change management team or group, sharing success stories, coaching and reinforcing successful efforts.

Source date: 2007

## What would you do differently the next time on a change management deployment?

Participants also provided a number of suggestions for what they would do differently on their next change management deployment effort. While many ideas were provided, four main themes emerged:

1. **Effective sponsorship**
The change management deployment initiative needed to have a designated and appropriate sponsor. Additional sponsorship should come from across the organization and from the business. Sponsors were key in showing that the organization was committed to change management.

2. **Structure for deployment initiative**
There were many suggestions for bringing more structure to the deployment initiative. Structure included a systematic plan developed ahead of the rollout, a more strategic approach and formal assessments of the size of the effort and the current gaps

(where are we today with change management compared to where we want to be).

3. **Appropriate resources and budget**
The change management effort needed appropriate resources to be effective including appropriate budget, time and team members to work on the initiative.

4. **More effective training**
More training was needed, and the training program should be formalized and reach across the entire organization. Several participants suggested making change management part of the existing supervisory skills and training program.

Source date: 2007

## Group dedicated to change management deployment

Two thirds of study participants indicated they were working to deploy change management throughout the organization. Figure 46 shows the percentage of this subset that had a group or individual dedicated to deploying change management across the organization. Nearly two thirds of participants actively working to deploy change management had an individual or group dedicated to this effort.

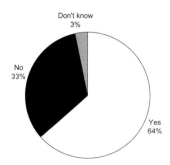

**Figure 46 – Participants with group dedicated to change management deployment**

Two thirds of participants reported having teams of five or fewer people working on change management deployment.

## Location of change management group

Participants who were working to deploy change management throughout the organization were asked to comment on where in the organization they were currently located, and where they may be better positioned going forward.

Figure 47 shows the results for where change management resided in the organization. As in the 2007 study, Human Resources was the most common response for where the change management group was placed, again with nearly one quarter of responses.

Information Technology was sixth on the list in 2007 but moved up to second on the list in 2009. The Project Management Office, an independent office or group, and Organization Development filled out the top five locations.

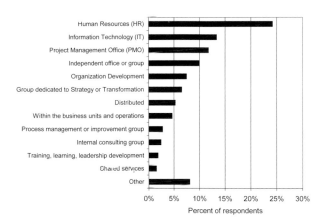

**Figure 47 – Where does the change management group reside in the organization?**

For the first time, the 2009 study also included questions on where the change management group should reside in the organization and why. Figure 48 shows the top eight responses to this question. The Project Management Office was

identified as the best location for the change management group.

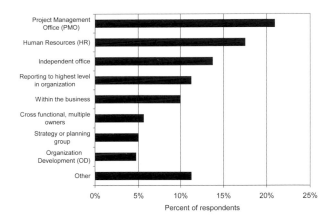

**Figure 48 – Where should the change management group reside?**

Participants offered up a number of reasons why the **Project Management Office** was the best place for change management. The most commonly cited reasons included:

- Alignment with and visibility into a majority of the change efforts underway

- Change management could be easily integrated into the project activities and the project methodology

- The group was already familiar with using methodologies and processes in relation to change efforts

- The PMO had clout, credibility and influence in the organization

- Change management could be more easily engaged early in the project life cycle

- The PMO offered some independence from the operational issues that may divert focus from the given change

The second most frequently cited location for change management was in **Human Resources** for the following reasons:

- HR and change management both focus on the people side of the organization

- Typically, HR touched the entire enterprise and reached across multiple divisions or business units

- Other activities and knowledge that closely aligned with change management resided in HR, including Organization Development, training and communications

- Staff were more easily influenced by HR

- HR already had a good "pulse" of the workforce

The third most frequently cited location for change management was an **independent office or group,** sometimes referred to as the Change Management Office. Participants cited the following benefits:

- No biases to particular changes, departments or divisions

- Effort on change management was focused

- Executive buy-in and commitment was demonstrated by having an independent office

- More easily took an enterprise view of the changes underway

- Enabled application to both project and non-project changes

Many participants who indicated an independent office did comment on the importance of staying connected with other groups working on change, including HR, the PMO and the IT organization.

Number four on the list was reporting directly to the **highest level** in the organization. The reasons for this location included:

- Visible sponsorship and commitment to change management

- Built-in access to sponsors on key initiatives

- Not being "bogged down" by operational issues and departmental resistance

- Ability to connect to strategy

Some participants suggested a **cross-functional model** or multiple owners. They commented on the importance of a network dedicated to change

management throughout the organization. Typically, the owners included some combination of: HR, the PMO, OD and IT.

Participants who indicated a **strategy or planning group**, such as Strategic Planning or Corporate Strategy, felt that this location provided the change management group with the best access to the most important projects in the organization. This group also typically reported to a very senior manager.

The participants that indicated **Organization Development (OD)** said that this group had broad visibility across much of the organization and had credibility and history working with large scale changes.

"Other" responses included:

- Internal consulting group

- Information Technology (IT)

- Centralized core team with representation in the business

- Operations

- Groups dedicated to performance improvement

- Training or Leadership Development

## Messages from executives about the need for change management

Participants were asked to share the messages their leaders had delivered to their organizations about the need for change management, including:

- **Messages about "change" in general**
  o Change is necessary and needed
  o The organization must respond faster
  o Change is required to remain competitive
  o Change will happen continually
  o Change is here to stay
  o Change is healthy and means progress

- o   Be ready for constant changes

- **Advantages of change management**

  - o   Change management is vital to the success and survival of the organization

  - o   Change management means growth and achieving goals in the future

  - o   Change management is an important element of projects and helps them be successful

  - o   Change management drives project outcomes

  - o   Change management has been successful and delivered results

  - o   Change management is needed to serve customers and the marketplace

- **Expectations of future behaviors**

  - o   Projects will need a change management plan developed at the beginning of the project

  - o   Everyone needs to take part

  - o   Change management is "everyone's job"

  - o   The organization is adopting a common approach to change management

  - o   Change management takes time and resources, but is worth it

Source date: 2007

# Change saturation and portfolio management

## *Level of saturation*

There was an increase in the percentage of participants who indicated that their organization was nearing, at or past a point of change saturation in 2009 as compared to 2007 (Figure 49). In total, two thirds of participants indicated their organization was nearing, at or past the point of change saturation. The percentage of study participants who indicated their organization was past the point of saturation increased from nearly 15% to nearly 18%. The largest increase was in participants reporting that they were nearing the point of change saturation, from 22% in the 2007 study to over one quarter (27%) in the 2009 study.

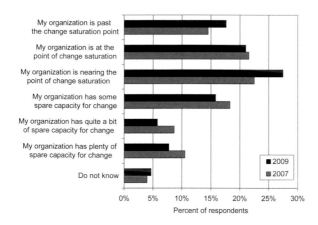

**Figure 49 – Current levels of change saturation**

## *Change expected in next two years*

In addition to reporting on the current level of change saturation, participants provided data on the amount of change they expected in their organization in the next two years (Figure 50). Over three quarters of participants (76%) expected an increase in the amount of change over the next two years.

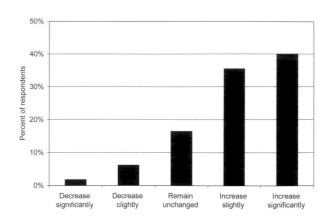

**Figure 50 – Amount of change expected in the next two years**

## *Identifying change saturation*

Participants were asked how they identified when change saturation was occurring. Most participants shared the symptoms they could observe in a change saturated workplace. A small group of participants also shared proactive approaches they took to monitor saturation levels.

For those participants who took proactive steps to monitor change saturation, the following approaches were cited:

- Feedback gathered directly from employees and managers on their perception of the level and amount of change that was occurring

- Surveys and interviews that included questions on the amount of change, including small group sessions and satisfaction surveys

- Active management of project resource allocation and scheduling, including the use of mapping tools and Enterprise Project Management (EPM) tools

- Assessments of the changes and the impact they would have by group or stakeholder

- Evaluation of the number of change efforts underway

- Reporting by project teams and change management teams

- Assessment of the time available to handle change at the employee level

- Assessment of success rates of change efforts over time, taking into consideration the amount of change happening in the organization

- Comparative observation evaluating the amount of change happening and the level of discontent in different parts of the organization

In terms of the impacts of change saturation that participants observed in their organization, the responses fell into three categories:

1. Individual symptoms

2. Organizational symptoms

3. Project symptoms

**Individual symptoms:**

- Disengagement, apathy and indifference – employees were not motivated to take part in the change or in their work and in some instances they began to shut down; a number of participants also cited a lack of questions and a lack of resistance as indicators of disengagement

- Burn out and fatigue – employees were visibly tired

- Anxiety, stress and weariness

- Confusion – about both the changes and the direction of the organization

- More complaints and "noise"

- Employees became desensitized, numb and lethargic

- Frustration

- Overloaded and feeling overwhelmed

- Cynicism and skepticism

- Anger – including more aggressive behaviors and quicker tempers

- Complacency

**Organizational symptoms:**

- Automatic resistance – employees reacted to any type of change with immediate resistance, no matter what the particulars of the change were

- Lack of focus on operations – participants cited productivity declines, "business as usual" tasks being ignored, issues not being addressed, a lack of flow, quality issues and difficulty in prioritizing work

- Attrition and turnover – valued employees left the organization

- Low morale throughout the organization

- Flavor of the month mentality – changes were constantly being introduced but not followed through to conclusion

- Absenteeism increased

- A lot of work being done but no progress or real change taking hold

- "Wait it out" mentality where employees simply ignored a change and hoped it would go away

- Changes were viewed as distractions

**Project symptoms**

- Lack of necessary resources for projects, including budget and people

- Poor project delivery including failure to produce expected results

- Delays and schedule implications, including slowed progress and missed deadlines

- Little direction and sponsorship from senior leaders

- Competition and conflict between projects

- Inability to finish out projects as the next change is started before the last one is solidified

- Non-compliance by employees including lower adoption levels and requested changes being completely ignored

- Team members stretched too thin and working unmanageable amounts

- Project activities not occurring

## *Tactics for coping with saturation*

Participants provided a number of tactics for addressing change saturation. The most frequently cited techniques for dealing with periods of excessive change were:

1. **Establish and communicate priorities**
   By an overwhelming margin, participants commented on the need to set project priorities to alleviate change saturation. Priorities should be set by senior leaders. Once priorities were established, they needed to be communicated to the rest of the organization.

2. **Communicate effectively**
   Communications should be from multiple sources in the organization. It should be frequent, consistent, focused and should show how changes fit into the strategy. Additionally, participants stated that it was important to communicate a vision of the future or the "big picture" for the organization. Communications should also include soliciting feedback.

3. **Celebrate and reward success**
   During times of change saturation, it was increasingly important to focus on successes. Participants particularly noted that quick wins must be celebrated to create momentum.

4. **Clearly demonstrate why the changes are needed**
   Not understanding the reasons for change was cited as the number one overall reason for resistance. In times of change saturation, creating a clear and compelling case for change was even more important.

5. **Create the expectation that change is constant**
   One way of dealing with change saturation is to create the expectation with employees that business now requires constant change, and it should be expected and prepared for.

6. **Involve employees early in changes**
   Involving employees earlier in changes, during the up-front design work, created buy-in and ownership that could help employees when they were facing a large number of changes.

7. **Create appreciation of change saturation**
   Participants suggested creating a mapping of projects and impacted groups to build a better understanding and appreciation for the saturation that was occurring. Additionally, several mentioned the importance of creating this understanding at the senior leadership level.

8. **Empathize with employees**
   Acknowledge the fact that there is tremendous change happening in the organization, that managers and leaders know it is difficult and that employees are not alone. Showing employees that senior managers "see and appreciate" the amount of change was also cited.

### Project governance changes
In addition to the suggestions above, many participants provided comments on the actual management of the projects underway. Suggestions related to project governance included:

- Stagger or sequence changes

- Break changes into segments or phases

- Reduce number of initiatives

- Slow the pace of change

- Cut non-value-added or less important projects to reduce clutter

- Ensure that changes align with strategy

- Consolidate similar projects

- Create collaboration and coordination between projects

- Take on smaller but more frequent changes

- Set and maintain project scopes

- Increase control of new project launches

Source date: 2007

## *Inventory and portfolio management processes*

Participants in the 2009 study indicated whether they kept an inventory of all of the changes underway and if they had a structured process for managing the portfolio of change in the organization. Over one third of participants kept an inventory or list of all of the changes underway (Figure 51), while just under one quarter of participants (24%) had a structured process for managing the portfolio of change (Figure 52).

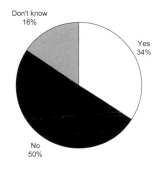

**Figure 51 – Kept an inventory of all changes underway**

Participants indicated who in the organization maintained the list or inventory of changes underway. The most common responses were:

- Project Management Office (PMO)

- Senior leadership – including a particular member of the C-club (CEO, COO, CFO, CIO), an executive team or staff members of senior leaders

- Change Management Office, group, team or council

- Distributed – department leaders kept their own inventory

- Strategy and Planning – including Office of Strategic Management, Strategic Planning Office or Business Planning Team

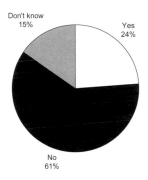

**Figure 52 – Have a structured process for managing the portfolio of change**

## *Tactics for managing the portfolio of change*

For the first time, participants in the 2009 study were asked to identify the tactics they used to manage the portfolio of change – the collection of all change efforts underway. A small number of participants (approximately 6% of responses) indicated that they were taking steps toward portfolio management. The top approaches for managing the portfolio of change were:

1. **The use of tools to show the portfolio**
   These responses included a list or log of initiatives, a change dashboard, a central database of project plans, a vendor-provided tool, resource and time tracking tools, change impact maps and change calendars.

2. **Centralized planning by a project-focused body**
   Responses included a project office, a program office, a project committee or a steering group.

3. **Regular meetings**
   These were typically held monthly or quarterly to review status and progress.

4. **Senior leadership meetings and discussions**
   Executive meetings focused on the portfolio of change.

5. **Processes for managing project progress**
   These included prioritization tools and approval gates, demand management processes, planning and budgeting exercises that included multiple projects.

6. **Strategic planning oversaw the portfolio**
   Portfolio discussions included in the annual planning process and the use of a strategic project list or Office of Strategic Management.

7. **Dedicated group or resource**
   An employee or group of employees tasked with managing the portfolio of change.

## Resolving project conflicts

Participants were asked how their organization resolved conflicts between projects when there was competition for resources, budget or impact on people in the organization. By a fairly large margin, the two top responses were prioritization and senior leadership decisions and resolutions. The top approaches for resolving project conflicts were:

- **Prioritization**
  The top response for resolving project conflicts was returning to some sort of prioritization process. Typically, prioritization took place ahead of the project launches and involved certain criteria for comparing projects to one another. The most frequently cited prioritization criteria included:

  o Highest value, benefit, impact or expected ROI for the organization

  o Strategic alignment and importance to the business

  o Business urgency

  o Regulatory or legislative mandates

- **Senior leadership decisions and resolutions**
  The second most-cited approach included the involvement of senior leaders. In some cases, decisions were simply made by the CEO, while in other cases this involved discussions with senior management teams. A number of participants indicated that when conflict did arise and could not be sorted out, the issue was escalated to senior management for resolution.

- **Use of boards and oversight committees**
  A number of participants indicated that project conflicts were addressed by the collaborative work of an oversight group. Participants shared a number of names for this group including: steering group, steering committee, management review board, project control board, business exchange team, change control board and advisory board. Regardless of the name, this group had visibility across multiple projects and made decisions to resolve conflict.

- **Coordination by the PMO**
  The fourth most cited response was oversight by the Project Management Office (PMO). In some instances, a project portfolio office existed within the PMO to coordinate the different projects and their requirements for time, human resources and budget.

- **Negotiation**
  Some participants said that conflict was resolved directly by the teams and sponsors of the projects through a negotiation process.

- **Meetings and discussions**
  A less formal tactic for resolving conflicts was the use of face-to-face meetings and discussions with project teams, leaders and representatives from the business.

A number of participants cited the role of individuals in influencing decisions when conflict occurred. Responses here related to politics, the use of influence and clout resulting in projects moving forward. Several participants also cited, with a negative connotation, that the loudest people were the ones who were heard – a "squeaky wheel" approach. Finally, several participants indicated that projects with the strongest sponsor were favored in times of conflict.

## Number of major initiatives underway

Participants indicated the number of major initiatives underway in their organization at the current time (Figure 53). Nearly half indicated there were less than five major initiatives underway, while over 20% indicated that there were more than 20 major initiatives occurring in their organization.

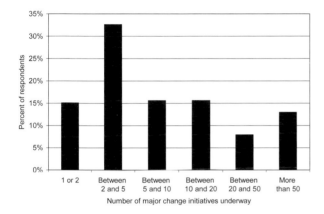

**Figure 53 – Number of major initiatives underway**

# Change management trends

## *Top ten trends in change management*

Participants in the 2009 study identified the trends they had seen in "change management" in their organization.

By nearly a two-to-one margin, the top trend was a greater awareness of the need for change management, mirroring the results in the 2007 study. The second most cited trend, again by a fairly significant margin, was the building of change management competencies across the organization. The top ten trends identified by 2009 participants were:

1. **A recognition of the need for change management**
   Overall, participants saw a greater understanding of and appreciation for the role of change management. Organizations and project-focused employees saw change management as important and as a needed aspect of any change project. Change management was identified as a key contributor to project success. There was a wider appreciation of the role change management played in contributing to return on investment (ROI) and benefit realization of projects; it was viewed as essential. A number of participants also commented on the growing interest and attention by senior leaders.

   *"Awareness that change management is an important success factor for project management."*

   *"Growing recognition of importance to successful ROI."*

   *"Acknowledgement that the investment in change management on the front end of a project will pay off in the end."*

2. **Change management competency building**
   Viewing change management as an emerging and necessary competency moved up from number five on the trends list in 2007 to number two in the 2009 study. Participants indicated more demand for training and knowledge around change management, as well as more widespread competency building programs. Change management competencies were becoming evident in senior leadership levels and front-line management levels.

   *"Recognition of managing and leading employees as a leadership capability."*

   *"Growing awareness of relatively new competence."*

   *"Appreciation of specific change skills."*

3. **Dedication of resources for change management**
   Participants identified the use of dedicated resources focused on change management as a key trend in their organization. Project leaders were more likely to appoint change management resources to support their change initiative, and change management specialists were being identified and developed within the organization.

4. **Use of change management tools**
   The fourth most-cited trend was a greater adoption of change management tools, processes and methodologies. Participants indicated that change management and its application was becoming more consistent and formalized in their organization. The use of more structured and formal processes was number two in the list of trends in the 2007 study.

   *"The appetite for a methodology is increasing."*

5. **Application of change management on projects**
   Participants commented that change management resources were now sought out by project teams, rather than looking for projects to support as they had done in the past. Project teams were bringing change management resources on board earlier in the project, during the planning phase, and were considering people-side issues earlier.

Several participants indicated that change management had become a requirement and that no major projects moved forward without change management.

*"We are being asked to join projects rather than asking."*

*"People have started accepting the behaviour change as [a] key ingredient for project planning."*

6. **Project management and change management integration**
Integration of change management and project management moved down several spots from the 2007 study in the list of top trends. Participants commented on the partnership, alignment and involvement in the planning process that was taking place with the project management and change management functions.

7. **Change saturation**
As evidenced by other findings in the study, organizations were increasingly facing a point of change saturation. The recognition of this condition and an increasing pace of change were highlighted as emerging trends. One participant noted the "change avalanche" the organization was experiencing.

8. **Standard change management approach**
More organizations were establishing a standard change management methodology for the entire enterprise.

9. **Establishment of a change management group**
Some organizations were creating and staffing a change management function in the organization, sometimes called the Change Management Office (CMO). Advances were made in staffing this group which centrally supported change management and change management training efforts. A number of participants indicated they were currently trying to decide where this group would reside in the organization.

10. **Management of the portfolio of change**
Several participants indicated that their organizations were making progress in understanding the people impact across the multiple projects underway. Participants mentioned steps including managing the portfolio of change, tracking projects, mapping future changes and prioritizing projects based on the change load.

The top trends in the 2007 report were:

1. A recognition of the need for change management
2. More structured and formal processes
3. Better understanding of what change management really is
4. Integration with project management
5. Recognition of change management as a new competency
6. Creation of formal job roles and titles
7. Earlier application on projects

# Participant demographics

## *Geographic representation*

Participants in the 2009 benchmarking study represented 65 countries from across the globe. Figure 54 below shows the geographic distribution of the last four benchmarking studies.

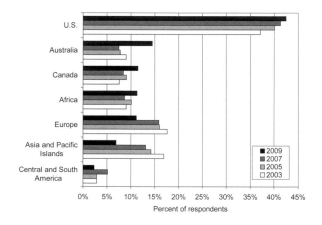

**Figure 54 – Geographic distribution of study participants**

## *Role of participants*

The role of participants in the 2009 benchmarking study is shown in Figure 55. The top three roles were: change management team leader, external consultant and project team leader.

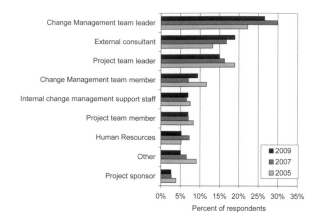

**Figure 55 – Role of participants**

## *Industry representation*

Figure 56 shows the industry representation in the 2009 benchmarking study. Industries represented by less than 2% of total study participants were included in the "Other" category. The top five industries were the same as in 2007, although "Consulting" and "Government – State or Local" both moved up one spot in the list.

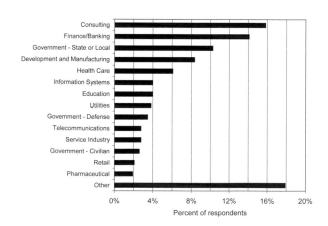

**Figure 56 – Industry segment**

## Size of organization

Participants in the 2009 study represented a wide range of organizations based on overall organization size (Figure 57). The largest participation came from organizations with more than $5 billion in annual revenue. Organizations with annual revenue of less than $10 million made up the second largest group.

Overall, organizations represented in the 2009 study were fairly similar in size to those in the previous studies.

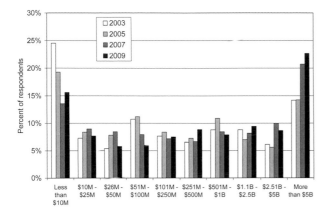

**Figure 57 – Size of organization (annual revenue)**

# Project profiles

## *Project stage*

Seventy percent of participants reported on projects that were in the implementation phase or completed, up from 65% in 2007 and 60% in 2005 (Figure 58).

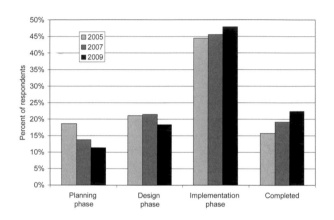

**Figure 58 – Project stage**

## *Project type*

As in previous studies, most projects involved changes to processes, systems, organization structures and job roles, as shown in Figure 59.

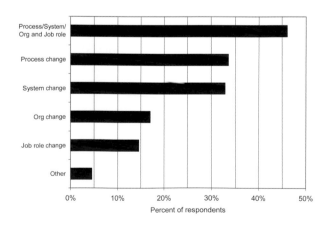

**Figure 59 – Project type**

Editor's note: Participants were able to select multiple responses, resulting in a total greater than 100%.

Nearly half of participants, 46%, had projects which impacted all of these factors. Projects involving staff reduction increased in the 2009 study, from 12% in 2007 to 26% in 2009.

## *Size of change*

Participants provided several data points on the size of the project on which they reported. Participants reported on:

- Scope of the change
- Project investment
- Number of employees impacted

### Scope of the change

Projects in the 2009 study had smaller scopes than in previous studies (Figure 60). In the 2009 study, only 44% of projects impacted the entire enterprise, compared to over 50% in the last three studies. Projects impacting multiple divisions increased from 15% of study participants in 2007 to 20% of study participants in 2009.

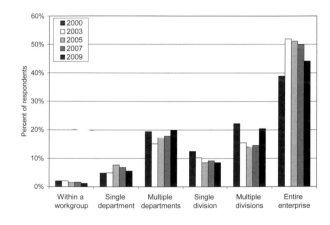

**Figure 60 – Scope of the change**

## Project investment

While project scope decreased slightly overall, the investment being made in the projects reported on in the 2009 study increased over the 2007 study. As shown in Figure 61, projects with investments of more than $10 million USD increased to 21% in 2009 from 18% in 2007. An even larger increase occurred in projects with investments between $1 million USD and $5 million USD, from 17% of participants in the 2007 study to 22% in the 2009 study. Representation from projects with investments of less than $1 million USD decreased in the 2009 study.

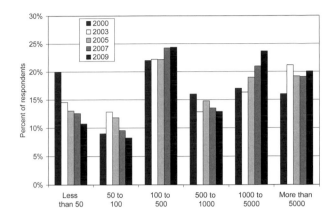

**Figure 62 – Employees impacted**

## *Meeting project objectives, schedule and budget*

For the second time, participants indicated to what degree their projects were meeting objectives, staying on schedule and staying on budget. Participants were also able to select "too early to tell" for each of the three project result questions.

### Meeting project objectives

Projects in the 2009 study performed better than those in the 2007 study (Figure 63). Specifically, 64% of projects met, exceeded or greatly exceeded objectives in the 2009 study, compared to 58% in the 2007 study. However, there was a smaller percentage of study participants who indicated exceeding or greatly exceeding objectives in the latest study.

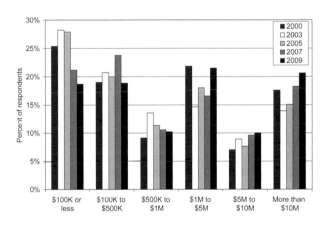

**Figure 61 – Project investment**

## Employees impacted

Figure 62 shows the breakdown of the number of employees impacted by the projects that were reported on in the 2009 benchmarking study. While the representation in the 2009 study remained fairly close to recent studies, there was an increase in representation from projects that impacted between 1000 and 5000 employees.

Responses for more than 5000 employees were further broken down in the 2009 study. Of the 20% of study participants reporting projects that impacted more than 5000 employees, 40% impacted between 5000 and 10,000 employees; 15% impacted between 10,000 and 20,000 employees and 45% impacted more than 20,000 employees.

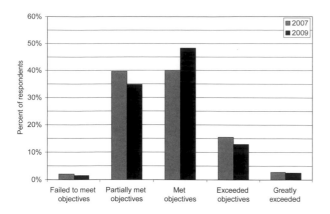

**Figure 63 – Meeting objectives**

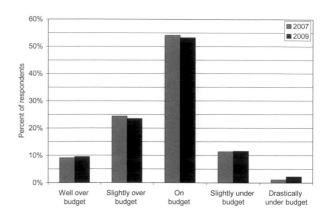

**Figure 65 – Projects on budget**

## Staying on schedule

Figure 64 shows the percentage of study participants indicating whether they were on or ahead of schedule. In the 2009 study, 45% of participants were on or ahead of schedule compared to 44% in the 2007 study.

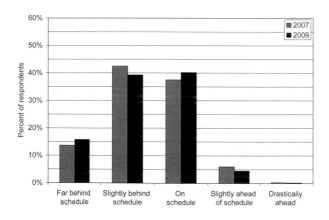

**Figure 64 – Projects on schedule**

## Staying on budget

Responses for projects on or under budget were similar to the 2007 study results (Figure 65). In both studies, two thirds of participants reported being on or under budget. Over half of participants reported being on budget.

## *If your project failed or only partially met objectives, what obstacles did you encounter?*

Study participants whose projects failed or only partially met objectives reported obstacles in one or more of the following areas:

1. Leadership and sponsorship
2. Project management
3. Change management

### 1. Leadership and sponsorship obstacles:

- Slow decision making by the sponsor
- Lack of involvement of key business leaders; difficulty getting all key stakeholders on board to build the necessary sponsor coalition
- Wavering support for the change; shifting or conflicting priorities of business leaders and managers
- Competing initiatives (too many projects going on at the same time)
- Insufficient resources or funding allocated to the project
- Insufficient visibility and communication from the sponsor
- Sponsor changed mid-project; lack of consistent leadership for this change

## 2. Project management obstacles:

- Project changed or expanded in scope (scope creep)

- Poor estimation of the project's magnitude; insufficient details to plan properly

- Unrealistic schedule from the planning process

- Poor project management throughout the project; failure to report progress honestly

- Inadequate management of vendors; development was behind schedule or vendors did not meet commitments

- Insufficient resources or lack of the correct resources for the project

- Poor quality deliverables from vendors, specifically around the release of new technology

- Poor assumptions about project's impact on the organization

- Lack of a solid business case for change

## 3. Change management obstacles:

- Employee resistance to the change; lacked buy-in and involvement

- Middle managers resisted the change

- Insufficient change management resources for the size of the change

- Underestimated the impact this change would have on employees

- Did not provide sufficient training to employees

- Poor communication about the project

- Lacked a formal change management process

\*\*\*

# Appendix A – 2009 study participant list

- 3rd i Consulting
- A.C.T. Advanced Consulting and Training
- Abbott Labs
- ABC (Australian Broadcasting Corporation)
- Absa Bank Ltd
- ABSA, division of Barclays
- Accretive Solutions
- Adams-Gabbert & Assoc., LLC
- ADP Inc
- Adult Multicultural Education Services (AMES)
- AEROFLOT Russian Airlines
- AFMC/A2
- Africa Crisis Management Team
- AHM
- Alberta Justice and Attorney General
- Alex Apouchtine
- ALTEC Training Centers
- Ambuja Realty Group
- Amertron Global
- Anderson Alliance Pty Ltd
- Applied Data Trends, Inc.
- Archstone Consulting
- ARGOS Consulting Group
- Artis Rei
- ASB, Auckland, New Zealand
- Ashland Inc.
- Astral Consulting Services
- AT&T
- Atos Origin
- Auckland City Council
- Australian Government Solicitor *
- Australian Human Service Organisation
- Avnet
- Bank of Canada
- Barnsley MBC
- Bartholomew Corporate Solutions p/l
- Bayer AG (The Bayer Group)
- BDM Directions
- BearingPoint
- Being Human
- Bell Canada
- BHP Billiton *
- Blue Oceans Information Solutions
- Blueshield of CA
- BMW Manufacturing
- Bombardier *
- Bonneville Power Administration *
- Booz Allen Hamilton *
- Bristol Myers Squibb
- British Telecommunications, Openreach division
- Brown-Forman Corporation
- BTS
- Bulyanhulu Gold Mine
- CA (Australia) *
- Comptroller and Auditor General of India
- California Manufacturing Technology Consulting
- CalPERS
- Canadian National
- Canadian Tire Financial Services
- CapGemini *
- Capita (National Strategies)
- Capital City Fruit
- Capital One
- Carbon Group *
- Cardinal Solutions Group *
- Caterpillar Inc. *
- CBA
- Central Bank of Nigeria
- Centre For Excellence, LLC
- Centre for Strategic Development
- Cetna Consulting Limited
- Chameleon Adventure Academy
- Change Consultoria
- Change Guides
- Change Management Consultants of Maryland, LLC
- ChangeWright Consulting
- Chevron *
- CIBC *
- Ciber Inc *
- Cirque du Soleil
- Cisco
- Citibank
- City and County of San Francisco
- City of Calgary
- City of Minneapolis
- City of Regina *
- City of Tacoma
- Clorox
- CMA Holdings Incorporated
- CMTC *
- Coaching Counts
- Coldwater Creek *
- Cole Consulting, LLC
- Commonwealth Bank
- Comptroller of the Currency (USA)
- County of Santa Clara
- Courtyard Group
- CPS Human Resource Services
- Croken Enterprises Inc
- Crystalmount Solutions Inc.
- CSIRO
- Cue 7 Consortium, Inc.
- Daar
- Dan Murphy's
- Danske Bank
- DBHG
- De Adviespraktijk
- Delaware Department of Insurance
- Delegata *
- Dell, Inc
- Deloitte Consulting
- Department of Correctional Service (South Africa)
- Department of Health and Human Services, Housing Tasmania *
- Department of Land Affairs (South Africa)
- Department of Planning and Economy (Abu Dhabi)

- Department of Treasury and Finance, Victoria, Australia
- Desjardins general insurance group
- Development Bank of Ethiopia
- Development of Malawian Enterprises Trust (DEMAT)
- Distinct Consulting
- District of Columbia Department of Small, Local Business Development
- Dreamhouse Consulting
- DSD Laboratories, Inc.
- Duke Energy
- EADS CASA
- Eastern Health
- EDS, an HP Company *
- EduServe/Amarillo College
- Egerton University
- Emerson Human Capital
- Enaxis Consulting, LP
- EnteGreat, Inc.
- Enteprise Community Partners, Inc.
- EQE Bulgaria AD
- Ergon Energy
- Erne Enterprise Ltd
- Esterline Defense Group
- Ethiopian Civil Service College [ECSC]
- Ethiopian Management Institute
- European Central Bank
- evolve! People and Process Management SA de CV
- Experian
- Farm Credit Canada
- Fireman's Fund Insurance Company
- Firestone International Associates, Inc.
- Focusphera Consulting
- Fonterra Brands Australia (P&B) Pty Ltd
- Fontys University
- Frank McGrath Change Management Ltd
- Freeman
- Friedkin Companies, Inc.
- Gambia Revenue Authority, Directorate Of Technical Services
- George Weston Foods Limited
- Georgia Technology Authority
- GHD
- GK Associates
- GlaxoSmithKline
- Goodwill Great Lakes
- Government Department (United Kingdom)
- Government of Canada
- Grupo Ultra
- GSI Group
- Guiness Ghana Breweries Ltd
- Gulf Water Company
- Harriss Wagner Management Consultants
- Hawassa University
- HBOS
- HCL Axon
- HD Supply
- HEC Paris
- High Plains Library District
- Hitachi Consulting *
- Housing Tasmania, Department of Health and Human Services
- HP Global eBusiness
- Humadyn-Center for Human Relations, Growth & Achievement
- Hungarian Foreign Trade Bank
- Hyosung Corporation
- IAT Program Management Office
- iB4e, Inc.
- IDC of South Africa Ltd
- Imagineering Solutions Inc.
- Impact Management Consultancy
- Incahoots Consultancy
- Infotek Systems
- Ink Business Development Services Ltd.
- Insurance Australia Group
- Intel Corporation
- Internal Revenue Service (USA)
- Inventure Solutions
- IPLAN
- J.R. Simplot Company
- Johnson & Johnson
- JP Morgan Chase
- Kansas Department of Revenue
- Keane Inc.
- Kenya Revenue Authority
- Kirsten Davies Consulting
- KPMG LLP
- Kusha Maadan Consulting Engineers (KMCE)
- La Société conseil Lambda inc
- Lakelanand HealthCare
- Leprino Foods
- Level 5
- LGFC
- LIBERTAS Zagreb - Business School of Economics
- Limited Brands
- Limpop Health Consortium
- Lions Clubs International, Multiple District 308
- LM Dulye & Co.
- Logisource
- Louisiana Machinery Co., LLC
- Lower Colorado River Authority (LCRA)
- MAC Carpet
- Maersk, Inc
- Dept. of Transport and Main Roads, Queensland
- Malawi Institute of Management
- Manship Associates
- MAP
- Marshall Manufacturing Co.
- Maryland Food Bank
- McKesson Canada
- McMaster University
- mdb Consulting
- Medavie Blue Cross
- Microsoft Corporation
- Milbank Manufacturing Company *
- Ministry of Education (Trinidad)
- MJ Medical
- MKR Consulting
- MMHE Sdn. Bhd.
- MOHSS
- Montana-Dakota Utilities
- Moshood Abiola Polytechnic
- Motorola
- Mutual of Omaha
- MWH Global *

- Namibia Institute of Pathology (NIP) Ltd
- NASA
- National City Corporation *
- Navistar, Inc.
- NCS Pte Ltd *
- Nedbank
- Nelson Consulting Group
- Network Rail Ltd
- New Brunswick Power Holding Corporation *
- New York State
- Nexen Inc.
- Nextant
- North Highland *
- NORTHPARK ZIM
- Oakton *
- OCBC
- Oklahoma Department of Human Services
- Online Business Systems
- Pacific Blue Cross
- Panduit Corp.
- Parramatta City Council
- PCGI Consulting Inc
- PeopleFirm, LLC
- PeopleNRG, Inc.
- Performance Path TM
- performanceglobal
- Philip Morris International
- Picourseware
- Plante & Moran, PLLC
- PMI Service Center Europe Sp. z o.o.
- POLITEC
- POQ
- Prime Therapeutics LLC *
- proacteur *
- PROJECT A LA CARTE, Inc.
- Projectology Pty Ltd
- Prominence Pty Ltd
- PT SOLTIUS Indonesia
- Qedis Consulting
- Quartzdyne Inc.
- Queensland Health
- RAAF
- Raiffeisen banka ad
- RAMSE Consulting
- Raytheon Company *
- RBC
- Reach Select
- Region of Peel
- Repars Inc
- Resources Global Professionals
- Rio Tinto - People and Organisational Support
- Robert Ayling Incorporated
- Roche *
- Rockwell Collins
- Roshcon / Highveld PFS
- RWD Technologies
- SAIC
- Saje Consulting
- Salalah College of Technology
- SAP Business Objects
- Saratoga Professional Services
- Sasol Technology *
- SATRENO AFRICA
- Satreno Change Management
- Satyam Computer Services
- Saudi Arabian Mining Company (Ma'aden)
- SBSA - Corporate and Investment banking
- SC COCA-COLA HELLENIC ROMANIA
- Scheltema & Co (Pty) Ltd
- Schneider National
- Schuyler County Community Services
- See Results, Inc.
- Sentry Insurance *
- Service Corporation International
- Severn Trent Water
- Shell *
- Shengquan Group
- Siemens Healthcare Diagnostics
- Sirius Solutions LLLP
- Solution Dynamics
- South Somerset District Council
- SouthWest Water Company
- Sovereign
- Spatial Information Services Pty Ltd
- Standard Bank of South Africa *
- State of Delaware *
- State of Nevada
- State Street Corp
- Stegmeier Consulting Group
- Sui Southern Gas Company
- SunTrust
- Symphini Change Management Inc.
- TASC Management Consulting, LLC
- TCWTUIF (Ethiopia)
- Teacher Training and Development (Botswana)
- Teched d.o.o.
- TechTeam Government Solutions *
- TEKsystems
- Tenaris
- Texas Childrens Hospital
- Textron, Change Management
- The Bremer Institute of TAFE
- The Dominion of Canada General Insurance Company
- The Hackett Group
- The Minto Group
- The New River Group
- The Student Loans Company Ltd
- Thomas Cook
- Thomson
- TMS Consulting
- Toyota Financial Services
- TradeDoubler AB
- Transnet
- Transocean
- Tri-Opus Technologies LLC
- tw telecom
- UCS
- Uganda Revenue Authority *
- UNISYS
- United Airlines, Information Technology Division
- United States Coast Guard
- University Hospital Maastricht
- University of Auckland *
- University of Ballarat
- University of Melbourne
- University of Southern Queensland

- University of Technology
- University of Tennessee Center for Industrial Services
- University of the West of Scotland
- University of Vermont
- Urbanizadora del Bajío, SA de CV
- UT Southwestern Medical Center
- Valsousa
- VeriSign
- Vertex Inc.
- VIP/Training
- Virginia Retirement System
- Wachovia Corporation
- WAPDA (Pakistan)
- Water Corporation of Western Australia
- Wawa, Inc.
- West Sussex County Council
- Whirlpool Corporation *
- World Omni Financial
- Wyeth
- Wyeth Pharmaceuticals
- Yarona Management Consulting
- Z. KefaLlinou & Co
- Zurich *

Names followed by an asterisk (*) had more than one individual participate in the study. Some organizations are not listed, per the specific request of a participant from that organization.

# Appendix B – 2007 study participant list

- 2020 Management Ltd.
- ABSA Bank Limited
- Accenture
- Acxiom Corporation
- Ada County Highway District
- Adaptis
- ADP
- Aegility.com
- Aflac, Inc.
- African Development Bank
- AFRICHANGE
- Albemarle Corporation
- Alcan
- Alchemists International*
- American Express Company
- ANZ Banking Group Limited
- Apis Consulting Group
- Appleton
- Applied Telemanagement Inc.
- Area Agency on Aging District 7, Inc.
- ARGOS Consulting Group
- Ascodi Services
- Associated Press
- Atos Origin
- Attorney General's Department of New South Wales
- Attorneys' Title Insurance Fund, Inc.
- Aurora Loan Services
- Australian Commonwealth Scientific and Industrial Research Organization (CSIRO)
- Australian Government Department of Finance and Administration
- Ayurvet Limited
- Bay Consulting Group
- Bell Aliant*
- BHPBilliton Iron Ore*
- Blue Cross Blue Shield of Michigan
- BlueOrange Consulting
- Blue Shield of California
- BMO Financial Group
- Boise Cascade
- Bombardier
- Booz Allen Hamilton*
- BP America Inc.
- Brisbane City Council*
- BT Group
- Bureau Veritas Group
- Buro Happold
- California Public Employees' Retirement System
- Caltex Australia Limited
- Canada Post Corporation*
- CapGemini
- CapGemini Italia
- Carbon Group Change Consultants
- Catalise*
- Caterpillar Inc.*
- Chait and Associates, Inc.
- ChangeWright Consulting
- Chery Automobile Co., Ltd.

- China Oxford Scholarship Fund
- Christensen/Roberts Solutions
- CIBC
- CIBER
- City of Boise, Idaho
- City of Edmonton
- City of Toronto
- City of Tshwane
- CK Consulting
- Clever Output Strategic Consulting
- Collin County Government
- Comenius University
- ConseQuent
- Consultus
- Co-operators General Insurance Company
- Corporate Systemics, Inc.
- Crawley Borough Council
- Crystal Lake Central High School
- CTG Health Care Solutions
- Datico
- DCP Midstream Partners, LP
- Defense Logistics Agency
- DeLaval Services LLC
- Derby Homes
- DeVry University
- DSD Laboratories
- EDS*
- Electric Insurance Company
- Engen Petroleum
- Entergy
- eProcesses Consulting
- Ergon Energy
- Ernst & Young
- ESNAAD
- Ethicon Endo-Surgery, Inc.
- Ethiopian Management Institute
- Etisalat
- Expressworks International
- Fairlead BVBA
- Farm Credit Canada*
- Fiberweb
- Financial Services Authority
- Firestone International Associates, Inc.
- First Data Corporation*
- Fontys University of Applied Sciences
- Ford Motor Company
- Forma Change Inc.
- Fujitsu Consulting*
- Fundacao Getulio Vargas
- GBM Corporación
- Getronics
- GKNM Hospital
- GlaxoSmithKline
- Government of Nova Scotia*
- Grupo Pão de Açúcar
- Hanover
- Harman/Becker Automotive Systems
- Harriss Wagner Management Consultants

- HCMC University of Technology
- HDR Inc.
- Hellmuth, Obata + Kassabaum
- Heron Advisory Group
- Hewlett-Packard
- Hi-Performance Learning
- Hitachi Consulting*
- HOK Visual Communications*
- Homeserve
- Honeoye Falls-Lima Central School District
- ICTS Global
- Impact Management Consultancy
- InfoChoice
- Infosys Consulting
- Inova Health System
- InSightec Ltd.
- Instituto de Logistica, S.C.
- Insurance Corporation of British Columbia
- Intel
- InterActive Financial Services Inc.
- Internal Revenue Service
- International Truck and Engine Corporation
- Isagen S.A.
- ITP New Zealand
- IUTUM
- JD Lowry Computer Service
- Jet Propulsion Laboratory
- JLT Mobile Computers
- Key Performance Consulting
- Kimberly-Clark
- KLA-Tencor
- L-3 Communications
- Laboratories Esteve
- Lascelles de Mercado & Co. Ltd.
- Leaders Training & Consultancy
- Leadership Intelligence Inc.*
- Lejara Enterprise Solutions
- Liberty Systems
- Limited Brands, Inc.
- Lion Nathan
- Liverpool John Moores University
- London Borough of Croydon
- MAC Carpet
- Make Change Positive, LLC
- Malaysia Marine and Heavy Engineering
- Massachusetts Convention Center Authority
- Medtronic, Inc.*
- Memorial Sloan-Kettering Cancer Center
- Middle East Contact Center Management Association
- Mississippi Valley Surgery Center
- MLP Consultants, LLC
- Molson Coors Brewing Company*
- Motorola, Inc.
- MUSE Consulting Inc.
- NASA
- National City Corporation*
- National Defense and Canadian Forces*
- Nelson Consulting Group
- Neoris Consulting Services
- Nestle
- Nevada Division of Child & Family Services
- North Highland
- NorthKey Community Care
- North-West University
- OCBC Bank
- Old Mutual plc
- Option One Mortgage Company
- Oregon Department of Transportation
- Pacific Gas & Electric Company
- PartyLite
- People and Process Management S.A. de C.V.
- Peoplematters
- PETROTRIN*
- Philippine Airlines
- Pier 1 Imports
- Plus Human Resources
- Pomeroy IT Solutions
- PricewaterhouseCoopers
- proacteur
- Prominence Pty Ltd
- Qedis Consulting
- Queensland Homicide Victims' Support Group
- RAMSE Consulting
- RBC Financial Group
- Results Kurumsal Verimlilik
- Reuters
- Rich Products Corporation*
- RWD Technologies
- SAIC
- SAJE Consulting
- Saline Water Conversion Corporation
- Sanofi-aventis
- SaskTel
- Sasol Infrachem
- Satyam Computer Services Ltd.
- Schneider Electric
- Sentry Insurance
- Serco Consulting
- SERVICOM
- Severn Trent Water
- Shakti Masti Overseas Pvt. Ltd.
- Shell Canada
- Shell*
- Silterra Malaysia Sdn Bhd
- Simeka BSG
- Sinclair-Cockburn Financial Group
- Skanska Brasil
- Soltius Indonesia
- South Carolina Department of Parks, Recreation & Tourism
- Southern California Edison
- Spirit Aerosystems, Europe
- Sprint Nextel
- Standard Bank of South Africa*
- State of Delaware
- Stegmeier Consulting Group
- Stored Energy Systems
- Student Loans Company Limited
- Sui Southern Gas Company Limited (SSGC)
- SunTrust Banks, Inc.
- SUPERA
- Swedish Social Insurance Agency
- Symantec
- TAM Iran Khodro
- TASC Management Consulting, LLC
- Tata Consultancy Services*

- Tata Sky
- Teched Consulting Services
- Technological University of Panama
- Tekla Corporation
- Tenaris
- Tennessee Valley Authority
- The Gillette Company
- The Hartford Financial Services Group, Inc.
- The Insolvency Service
- The Revere Group
- Theo Consulting Ltd.
- Transat A.T. Inc.
- Transformaciones Estrategicas
- Tri-Global Solutions Group Inc.
- Unisys
- United Nations
- United Nearshore Operations
- United States Army Reserve
- University of Bolton
- University of California - Davis
- University of Melbourne
- University of Paisley
- University of Texas Southwestern Medical Center
- University of Vermont
- Urbanizadora del Bajio
- Valsousa
- Vulcan Flight Management
- Wachovia Corporation*
- Warri Refining and Petrochemical Company
- Wayne County, Michigan
- Western Cape Education Department
- Western International Bank
- Whirlpool Corporation
- Wipro Technologies
- World Vision Inc.
- xwave
- Yucel Boru
- Zurich American Insurance Company

Names followed by an asterisk (*) had more than one individual participate in the study. Some organizations are not shown, per the specific request of the participant from that organization.

## About Prosci

Formed in 1994, Prosci is the leading provider of research and tools that enable organizations to manage the people side of change. As a research company, Prosci has conducted six longitudinal studies over the last eleven years to create the most complete body of knowledge available in the change management field. Research participants include more than 2000 organizations from 65 countries since 1998, including many of the largest companies and government organizations worldwide.

Prosci sponsors the Change Management Learning Center at **www.change-management.com**. This online resource provides access to Prosci's change management tools and a collection of books, articles, case studies and other change management resources. The nearly 40,000 registered members receive regular tutorials featuring the latest research and models in change management.

### Resources for the entire organization

Prosci has developed holistic models, processes and tools for effective change management. Prosci's ADKAR® Model and organizational change management methodology have become two of the most widely used approaches for managing the people side of change in corporations and government agencies. Prosci's change management approach provides a common language, customized tools and training for multiple levels in your organization:

**For change practitioners:**
Change Management Certification Program
*Change Management Toolkit*
Change Management Pilot or Pilot Professional

**For senior leaders and sponsors:**
Change Management Sponsor Program
*Change Management: the people side of change*
*Executive Guide to Change Management*

**For managers and supervisors:**
Change Management Coaching Program
*Change Management Guide for Managers and Supervisors*

**For employees:**
Change Management Orientation for Employees
*Employee's Survival Guide to Change*
ADKAR Worksheets

Prosci has also developed a licensing framework to enable organizations to deploy change management to all employees and to customize or tailor the materials to meet your specific needs. Contact Prosci for more information on licensing options and costs.

### Training

Prosci has been directly engaged in knowledge transfer and coaching of executives and project teams for very diverse groups, including many Fortune 500 companies and large government organizations. Prosci's popular Change Management Certification Program includes training credits from Colorado State University, the Project Management Institute® (PMI) and the Society for Human Resources Management (SHRM). Training programs are held onsite at client locations around the world and in open-enrollment public programs.

**Contact us**
Web:   www.change-management.com
Email:   changemanagement@prosci.com
Phone:   +1 970-203-9332

Prosci Research
1367 South Garfield Avenue
Loveland, CO 80537 USA